THE
NINJA
AND THEIR SECRET
FIGHTING ART

STEPHEN K. HAYES

TUTTLE Publishing

Tokyo | Rutland, Vermont | Singapore

Disclaimer: Please note that the publisher and author(s) of this instructional book are NOT RESPONSIBLE in any manner whatsoever for any injury that may result from practicing the techniques and/or following the instructions given within. Martial Arts training can be dangerous—both to you and to others—if not practiced safely. If you're in doubt as to how to proceed or whether your practice is safe, consult with a trained martial arts teacher before beginning. Since the physical activities described herein may be too strenuous in nature for some readers, it is also essential that a physician be consulted prior to training.

ABOUT TUTTLE
"Books to Span the East and West"

Our core mission at Tuttle Publishing is to create books which bring people together one page at a time. Tuttle was founded in 1832 in the small New England town of Rutland, Vermont (USA). Our fundamental values remain as strong today as they were then—to publish best-in-class books informing the English-speaking world about the countries and peoples of Asia. The world has become a smaller place today and Asia's economic, cultural and political influence has expanded, yet the need for meaningful dialogue and information about this diverse region has never been greater. Since 1948, Tuttle has been a leader in publishing books on the cultures, arts, cuisines, languages and literatures of Asia. Our authors and photographers have won numerous awards and Tuttle has published thousands of books on subjects ranging from martial arts to paper crafts. We welcome you to explore the wealth of information available on Asia at www.tuttlepublishing.com.

Published by Tuttle Publishing, an imprint of Periplus Editions (HK) Ltd.

www.tuttlepublishing.com

Copyright © 1981 Charles E. Tuttle Publishing Co. Inc.

Library of Congress Catalog Card Number 81050105

ISBN 978-4-8053-1430-2

21 20 19 18 17   5 4 3 2 1   1612MP
Printed in Singapore

TUTTLE PUBLISHING® is a registered trademark of Tuttle Publishing, a division of Periplus Editions (HK) Ltd.

Distributed by

North America, Latin America & Europe
Tuttle Publishing, 364 Innovation Drive
North Clarendon, VT 05759-9436 U.S.A.
Tel: 1 (802) 773-8930; Fax: 1 (802) 773-6993
info@tuttlepublishing.com
www.tuttlepublishing.com

Japan
Tuttle Publishing, Yaekari Building, 3rd Floor
5-4-12 Osaki, Shinagawa-ku, Tokyo 141 0032
Tel: (81) 3 5437-0171; Fax: (81) 3 5437-0755
sales@tuttle.co.jp; www.tuttle.co.jp

Asia Pacific
Berkeley Books Pte. Ltd.
61 Tai Seng Avenue #02-12, Singapore 534167
Tel: (65) 6280-1330; Fax: (65) 6280-6290
inquiries@periplus.com.sg; www.periplus.com

Indonesia
PT Java Books Indonesia, Jl. Rawa Gelam IV No. 9
Kawasan Industri Pulogadung, Jakarta 13930
Tel: (62) 21 4682-1088; Fax: (62) 21 461-0206
crm@periplus.co.id; www.periplus.co.id

To Carolyn and Ira
*who loved me enough to encourage me
to be exactly what I always wanted to be*

✦ *TABLE OF CONTENTS*

✦ LIST OF ILLUSTRATIONS

✦ PREFACE

Having spent one-third of my life practicing the Asian fighting arts, I was honored to be the first American ever accepted as a personal student by the headmaster of the last historically unbroken *ninjutsu* tradition in Japan. After my initial training sessions in the moonlit Japanese countryside, my feelings of being honored changed to a growing realization that I had at last found the ultimate fighting art and philosophical system for me.

In the winter of 1978, in the midst of my several years in Japan, I began writing this, my first book, documenting the original teachings of these ancient and undiluted warrior ways. All these decades later, I am still proud of this book. It continues to shine valuable illumination on this so often misunderstood martial art.

I must express my gratitude to Masaaki Hatsumi, thirty-fourth headmaster of the Togakure-ryu *ninja* tradition, for giving me exactly what I wanted those decades ago. I sought answers unheard of in the greater martial arts world I had deliberately left behind. I became part of the *ninja* dojo when there were just dozens of people training, years before this book and my others made Masaaki Hatsumi world famous and brought thousands of eager students to his door. What I wanted was the lore of the *ninja* and their secret fighting art. I was rewarded with knowledge impossible to find in the mainstream martial arts. My teacher granted that to me, though more often than not I had to steal his knowledge; I was shown a path and then challenged to figure out the secrets for myself if I could.

My thanks go out to the staff of the Iga-Ueno Ninja Museum for information on the military aspects of Iga Ryu *ninjutsu*. They were there for me in the years long before Iga-Ueno became a popular attraction for tourists. I appreciate their allowing me to photograph their displays and reproduce them in this book.

I also wish to thank Rumiko Urata for her long hours of assistance in translating obscure Japanese documents. Who would have guessed in the late 1970s that she would become my bride, and we would celebrate daughters and then grandchildren as the years unfolded?

I greatly appreciate the friendship and aid of Koyu Tanaka. He so generously helped me get established in my new home in Japan. Many were our late night conversations in my humble little house on the Edo River.

And lastly, a thank you nod to the late Charles E. Tuttle, who signed my original contract for this book. He got me started on this wild, twisted adventure that has been my life since those daring days back in the 1970s.

I should mention that in these pages I have done my best to recall my training and conversations as accurately as possible. The conversations have been translated from Japanese into English, and edited for continuity. I assume responsibility for any mistakes or misinterpretations.

—STEPHEN K. HAYES
StephenKHayes.com

In an era over eight centuries ago, when Japan was composed of many independent feudal states and war was frequent, Daisuke of the Togakure family once suffered heavy losses in battle. Retreating into the mountains, he came upon the teachings of the warrior-priest Kain Doshi. There in the fog-shrouded peaks of Iga Province, Daisuke studied long and hard a new art of combat, new ways to use the body and spirit, a new vision. From this mystic teaching he learned to move freely without being perceived, and how to work his will without action. With the knowledge of these secrets, Daisuke emerged from the mists of Iga the master of a new concept of accomplishment. Thus was born the legend of the shadow warriors of Togakure.

(From a tale of the origin of the Togakure-ryu ninja)

1 ✦ *PERSPECTIVE*

Woven into the rich fabric of Japanese cultural, political, and religious history is the story of an incredible art of espionage and individual combat. Its name is *ninjutsu* 忍術, the art of stealth, the way of invisibility, and its practitioners were the legendary spies and commandos of feudal Japan known as the *ninja* 忍者. Ninjutsu flourished amid the civil turmoil of the fourteenth through seventeenth centuries. During this period the art was refined into a deadly science, incorporating sophisticated techniques for warfare, intelligence gathering, and spiritual development. When the odds were unfavorable or dishonor threatened, the ninja could be hired to bring victory and restore the harmony of society through espionage or assassination. Often a few black-garbed ninja could do by subtle means what it would have taken hundreds of armored soldiers to accomplish. It was these exploits that gave rise to legends that are still popular in Japan today.

The ninja's guiding philosophy was to choose the dark, quiet, and subtle method over the bold, active, and forceful. In this way, the natural order of events was disturbed as little as possible. Suggestion took the place of force, deception replaced confrontation, and the adversary was guided into unknowingly doing the ninja's bidding instead of being crushed in humiliating defeat. This psychological slant characterized ninjutsu, and allowed the ninja to accomplish the most while expending minimum energy and exposing himself to the least amount of danger.

Its practitioners considered ninjutsu to be a comprehensive art for the attainment of their goals, "the art of winning." This approach required a graphic visualization of the goal and unswerving commitment to reaching it, all under the guidance of perfect moral judgment. The ninja were commoners, far below the exalted status of the samurai warrior class, and thereby free of the samurai's rigid code of honor and prescribed way of handling situations. The samurai had to balance the dual considerations of achieving his goal and maintaining the honor and prestige of the family name, whereas the ninja was able to concentrate his energy exclusively on the goal at hand, having no honor or name to protect. Because of this total commitment, the service of the ninja commanded a high price.

Women as well as men were trained in the complex art of ninjutsu. *Kunoichi* (female ninja) posing as dancers, entertainers, or servants were often used for observation or espionage inside the enemy camp. Many times female assassins were able to gain the confidence of their victims through beauty and charm when other means of attack had proven futile.

ORIGIN

Looking back over a thousand years of history, it is difficult to sort out fact from fancy. There is no documentary evidence to support any one theory of the birth of this obscure art. The stories of the superstitious tell of the ninja's descent from the *tengu*, terrifying long-nosed demons said to be half man and half crow, and supposedly possessed of the ability to alter the laws of nature and the workings of men's minds.

Probably closer to the actual playing out of history are scrolls

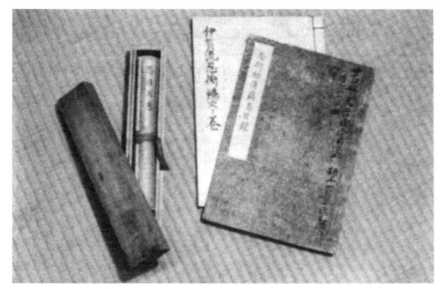

2. Ancient documents preserving the lore of the ninja.

3. Scroll depicting a ninja climbing tool.

indicating that the art had its ultimate source in military men who fled collapsing T'ang China around A.D. 900. When the mainland kingdoms that had employed them fell, generals and commanders such as Ikai, Cho Busho, and Cho Gyokko found themselves hunted men, and so sought sanctuary across the narrow sea on the islands of Japan. Their teachings found receptive ears and blended with the indigenous attitudes and approaches to warfare.

As well as Chinese military tactics there came the closely related teachings of Chinese mysticism, developed from the esoteric knowledge of India and Tibet. Chinese monks and shamans came to dwell in the forests and caves of the Kii Peninsula beginning about A.D. 1024. They expounded systems of integrated mind-body awareness, based on personal understanding of the order of the universe, which were taken up by the Japanese *yamabushi* (mountain warrior-priests), and *sennin* and *gyoja* (warrior-ascetics of the wilderness). Chinese mystic priests such as Kain Doshi, Gamon Doshi, and Kasumikage Doshi, as well as their Japanese disciples, are said to have been the teachers of the original ninja families. These beliefs remained closely associated with the ninja even after they became codified into the *mikkyo* (esoteric doctrine) sect of Buddhism in later years.

Ninjutsu coalesced gradually from a mixture of these Chinese and native Japanese elements; unlike most Oriental religions and martial arts, it was never actually founded at any one specific point in history. The basic body of knowledge that was later called ninjutsu was at first considered merely an unconventional way of looking at situations and accomplishing things. What went on to eventually become a highly systematic method of combat and espionage began as a shadowy counterculture, a reaction against the mainstream of Japanese political and social tradition.

For example, the ninjutsu *ryu* (tradition or school) of the Togakure family was not formalized until three generations after Daisuke Togakure began to develop it. Allied with a clan that was defeated in a series of battles against superior forces, Daisuke lost

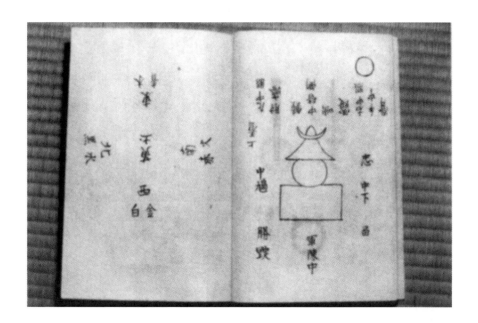

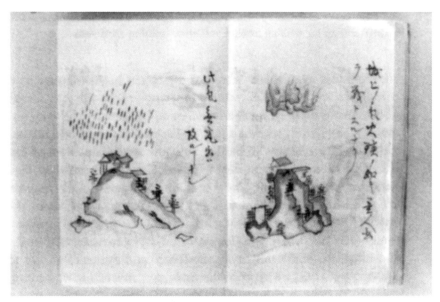

4, 5. Old books explaining ninja tactics and symbolism.

6. Instructions for making torches and other lighting apparatus.

all, including his samurai status, and escaped to the mountainous wilderness southeast of Kyoto. Wandering among the pine forests and marshes of the Kii Peninsula in 1162, he met the warrior-monk Kain Doshi, who had fled to Japan from the political and military upheaval in China. There in the mountain caves of Iga Province (within present-day Mie Prefecture), Daisuke studied with this mystic, learning new concepts of warfare and personal accomplishment based on Chinese and Tibetan ideas about the order of the universe. Daisuke was taught the practical applications of the balance of the elements in diet, in combat, in thought and emotion, and in utilizing the forces and cycles of nature to advantage. Thus, away from the limiting conventions of samurai conduct that he had never thought to question, he discovered a completely new way of working his will. It was Daisuke's descend-

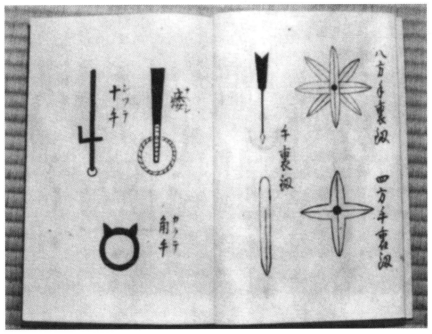

7. Old book showing ninja weapons.

ants that developed and refined these notions into the Togakure-ryu of ninjutsu, and came to be called by the name of ninja.

Most of the *ryu* of ninjutsu grew up in the mountains of south central Honshu island, including the two largest ones: the Iga-ryu and the Koga-ryu. The Iga-ryu, which like the Togakure-ryu operated in Iga Province, was under the control of the Momochi, Hattori, and Fujibayashi clans. The Koga-ryu, located in Koga Province (in modern Shiga Prefecture), took in 53 lesser-known families, including the Mochizuki, Ukai, Nakai, and many that adopted the name Koga.

There were also many smaller schools of ninjutsu, each with its own specialities, and each handed down through the members of a family that guarded its secrets with their lives. For example, the Koto-ryu specialized in techniques of bone breaking known

8. Shuriken.

as *koppojutsu*, which later evolved into jujutsu and karate. The Fudo-ryu relied heavily on *shuriken* (steel throwing blades) to hinder adversaries. A vast network of spies was maintained by the Kusunoki-ryu to gather and pass along information. The Kukishin-ryu developed many unorthodox methods of utilizing standard weapons of the period. The specialty of the Gyokko-ryu was the use of *koshijutsu*, the attacking of nerve centers with pinching or striking finger-drives. The Togakure-ryu's secret was the *shuko*, a spiked iron band worn around the hand, enabling the ninja to stop sword blades or climb trees and walls like a cat. Another device utilized by the Togakure ninja was the *tetsubishi*, a small spiked weapon used to slow pursuers or protect doorways. Made with spikes sticking out in all directions, the *tetsubishi* were scattered on the ground to be stepped on by the unsuspecting. In addition to these, dozens of other families such as the Taira, Izumo, Toda, Kashihara, Abe, Sakaue, and Mori were active in the secret arts collectively known as ninjutsu.

9. Shuko.

10. Tetsubishi.

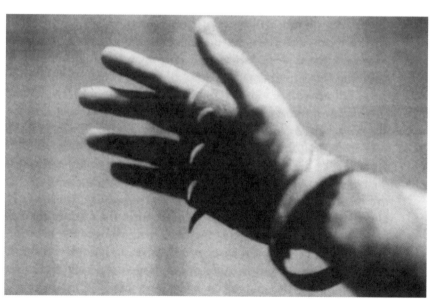

11. Wearing the shuko.

ORGANIZATION

As ninjutsu took form, the ninja developed an organizational system designed to preserve the essential element of secrecy. Three distinct ranks were established within the *ryu*, each rank with a specific type of work to do and specific responsibilities.

At the head of each *ryu* was a commander in chief known as a *jonin* (high man). The *jonin* controlled the activities of the ninja organization, and made the decisions about whom his ninja would aid and at what price. In the larger *ryu*, the *jonin* was a wise man who was well informed on all events in his area. His decisions were based on a philosophical understanding of the scheme of totality, and he was prompted to aid others by a concern for the right and the fitting. The true *jonin* was a maintainer of harmony, aiding the underdog faced with hopeless odds and no honorable recourse.

The *jonin* reduced his vulnerability by remaining anonymous to most of his agents. This made it impossible for the agents to reveal his identity under torture or in selling out to rival organizations. Furthermore, the *jonin* could assign several agents to the same mission without their knowledge, to prevent a double cross. By receiving bits of information from all of these agents, he became the only one with a complete picture of the situation. This system of invisible command is popular among many modern criminal organizations for much the same reasons.

Working for the *jonin* was a group of officers known as *chunin* (middle men). To this group fell the duties of actually organizing the operation decided on by the *jonin*. The *chunin* knew how to get the job done and which agents to assign to particular tasks. He also served as a buffer, carrying orders from the *jonin* to the field and thereby insuring the leader's safety and anonymity.

As an officer class, the *chunin* rarely took active roles as agents. Their training included some of the ninja's fighting techniques and espionage tactics, but strategy and effective management were the prime areas of concern.

The field agent was known as a *genin* (low man). He had the responsibility of carrying out the plans and operations of his superiors. It was this *genin* that inspired all the fantastic legends connected with the exploits of the ninja.

When not engaged in espionage, *genin* lived with their families in remote, secret villages, almost always located in hard-to-reach mountainous areas. Appearing to be farmers, the ninja could live and train without constantly being on guard. Because of the insulated system of organization, two groups of *genin* often had no idea that they were working for the same *jonin*.

TRAINING

Historically, ninjutsu was a profession inherited at birth. From infancy, the children of ninja families were conditioned to be constantly aware of the things around them. As they grew up, they were gradually educated in the secrets and traditions of the *ryu*. At age five or six, their play activities began to take the form of training exercises. Games stressing balance and agility were introduced. The children would walk atop narrow horizontal poles, run up inclined planks, and leap over low shrubs. At age nine, body conditioning for muscle limberness and joint flexibility was stressed. The children practiced rolling, jumping, and yoga-like movements. As the young ninja matured, striking and kicking techniques were practiced against targets of bundled straw. From this training the children progressed to the basics of unarmed self-defense techniques, and later to the fundamentals of using the Japanese sword and the traditional wooden staff.

In the early teen years, the ninja learned to use the special weapons of their *ryu*. Blade throwing, the concealment of weapons, and rope or chain techniques might be taught. They practiced swimming and underwater tactics, and learned how to use nature to gather information or conceal themselves. Hours were spent in confined quarters or hanging from trees to build patience, endur-

12. Ninja in training.

ance, and stamina. There were exercises in silent movement and distance running, and the ninja were taught to leap from tree to tree, and from roof to roof.

In the late teen years, ninja learned to be actors and practical psychologists. Through observation of their own actions as well as those of others, they came to understand the workings of the psyche, and how to use the mental weaknesses and limitations of others to their own advantage. The young ninja also learned how to prepare medicines and drugs. They were shown how to gain surreptitious entrance to buildings, and techniques for climbing walls, crossing ceilings, and stealing under floors. Ways of tying and binding the enemy as well as methods of escape were taught. The ninja also practiced sketching maps, routes and landmarks, and faces.

AT THE HEIGHT OF POWER

By the fourteenth century, the ninja had developed into powers in the areas of Iga and Koga. They worked to secure their own local influence, served as protectors of the *mikkyo* temples, and hired out their services to those who sympathized with their unconventional methods and life-style.

But as political turbulence and war increased after the battle of Onin no Ran in 1467, there was more call for the ninja's deadly skills throughout Japan. They were employed by powerful rulers such as Shogun (military dictator of all Japan) Yoshihisa Ashikaga, and many lesser warlords. The mystics of the mountains began to stress military tactics, and emerged as a force to be reckoned with. No longer content to remain aloof in their secret villages, performing at the whim of others, the ninja extended their own influence in Japan by assassinating hostile lords and attacking their forces.

One result of this increased activity was the blossoming of popular tales about the ninja, which portrayed them more as sorcerers than as commandos. Able to walk on water, pass through solid walls, read minds, know the future, disappear at will, or transform themselves into wolves or crows, the ninja of the sixteenth-century legends seemed fearsome and invincible foes to their adversaries.

The tales were the result of a mixture of imagination, exaggeration, and deception. The original ninja were mystics, in touch with powers that we would describe as psychic today. Their ability to tune into the scheme of totality and thereby become receptive to subtle input from beyond the usual five senses was strange and terrifying to the common foot soldier. Thus, confronted by a single ninja with fingers entwined in one of the mystic *kuji-in* (energy-channeling hand positions), a superstitious opponent might indeed feel weakened by his own subconscious fear. The opponent naturally attributed this weakness to ninja magic. Furthermore, by using their knowledge of the laws of nature and the character of an adversary to anticipate the outcome of a series of events, the ninja developed the reputation of being able to know and guide the future. Unique and imaginative weapons and tools, special methods of walking and climbing, and completely unorthodox combat techniques all intensified the awe in which the ninja were held.

THE DECLINE

The avowed enemy of all ninja was the powerful general Nobunaga Oda, infamous because of his high regard for forceful and usually violent action as a means of attaining his goals. A cold pragmatist, Nobunaga detested the mysterious and occult teachings of the ninja *mikkyo*, and even went so far as to protect and encourage the budding Christian religion in Japan to combat the influence of mysticism. The Christian church structure, with its hierarchy of European priests and bishops to control the followers, seemed ripe for use as a tool to Nobunaga. The esoteric ninja beliefs, in which every man was his own priest, were just an obstacle to the ambitious general's plans to become shogun.

Legend has it that while riding through Iga with his samurai one time, Nobunaga was thrown from his horse for the first time in his life. The haunting desolation of the eerie, fog-enshrouded forests of Iga, coupled with the unprecedented fall from his horse, planted in Nobunaga a feeling of apprehension that culminated in his ordering his son Katsuyori to attack the ninja stronghold.

13. One of the ninja's 81 mystic hand positions.

In the battle of Tensho Iga no Ran in 1579, Nobunaga's samurai troops under the command of Katsuyori were soundly defeated by ninja of Iga led by Sandayu Momochi. Infuriated, Nobunaga retaliated by himself leading a massive invasion of Iga in 1581. This time, outnumbered by more than ten to one, the men, women, and children of Iga were slaughtered by their enemies. The ninja, the legendary invisible ones, had been crushed by the brute force they so despised.

29

A few ninja survived, to scatter and go into even deeper hiding than before. Families like the Tarao, Hattori, Togakure, and Momochi took their remaining members and withdrew to regroup in new mountain retreats. The training of ninja slowly began again, and a new life unfolded for the outlaw families.

With the 1582 murder of Nobunaga in Honnoji, his ally Ieyasu Tokugawa had to move safely from Sakai in the Osaka area to his stronghold of Okazaki Castle near present-day Nagoya, without passing through the dangerous Honnoji territory. The only route left was through the treacherous mountains of Iga and Koga. Ieyasu left his fate in the hands of Iga-ryu ninja Hanzo Hattori. Hanzo successfully organized several *ryu* in Iga, as well as their one-time rivals in Koga, to afford protection and safe passage to the man who would become shogun in 1603 and whose family would rule Japan for the next two and a half centuries. Some of the ninja families were happy to assist Ieyasu, simply because of their joy at the death of Nobunaga. Some families saw it as a chance to secure a more stable future for themselves. Some remained silently apart from the action, keeping warily to themselves and neither attacking nor assisting.

Ironically, it was peace, not defeat in battle, that caused the final demise of the ninja clans. The rule of the Tokugawa shoguns —Ieyasu and his descendants—brought peace and civil order, which cut off demand for the ninja's services. With less opportunity for work in the *ryu*, many *chunin* and some *genin* struck out on their own, but without the philosophical direction of the *jonin* their wisdom and effectiveness declined. Some found applications for their unique talents in police work, and others in the military. Many turned to crime, so that the right amount of money, regardless of purpose, could hire men who had once been ninja, but had become mere thugs in ninja clothing. Others cut a more romantic figure as outlaws or guerrilla fighters. The deeds of ninja bandit-heroes such as Sasuke Sarutobi, Saizo Kirigakure, and Goemon Ishikawa are glamorized in the children's tales of Japan, just as

30

14. A modern reconstruction of the Hakuhojo (White Phoenix Castle) in Iga. The original castle was established in 1581 by a vassal of Nobunaga to help control the ninja; seized by the ninja after Nobunaga's death, it was later enlarged by Ieyasu, and destroyed by a typhoon in 1612.

the stories of Robin Hood, Zorro, and Butch Cassidy and the Sundance Kid are told in the Western world today.

After becoming shogun, Ieyasu hired a number of ninja and gave the Hattori family the job of organizing them into a secret police force to protect the ruler and his family members. Former

31

Iga and Koga ninja assumed the roles of gardeners and caretakers on the estates of the shogun and his chief retainers in order to be close at hand at all times. However, security and comfort brought about the downfall of the descendants of the original ninja. Without the threat of war or the need to employ ninjutsu skills, their role gradually declined over the years, until the men who had once been deadly ninja agents had deteriorated into little more than glorified security guards. Their pay was miserably low, their status was degrading, and their official duties were restricted to such activities as opening doors and posing as targets for snowballs thrown by the girls of samurai families.

The few ninja families that remained in the mountain wilderness outside the old capital of Kyoto shrouded themselves in total secrecy, staying completely concealed from the Tokugawa shoguns in their new capital, Edo (today's Tokyo). Meanwhile, the ninja under contract to the shoguns decayed into ineffectuality. The Shimabara rebellion of 1637–38, in which Christian peasants living near Nagasaki revolted against religious and economic oppression, provided an opportunity for the shogun's ninja to go back into action. A group of ten former Iga ninja, the oldest of whom was 63, was resurrected from decades of retirement and sent to the site of the battle to gather intelligence. The aged ninja were able to steal food supplies for the government troops, but since none of them were linguists, they were unable to imitate the Kyushu dialect necessary for slipping into the rebels' fortress and obtaining information. The mission was not considered successful, although the government troops did quell the rebellion.

The last activity of the Tokugawa ninja occured with the arrival of Commodore Perry's "black ships" in 1853. The ninja Yasusuke Sawamura was ordered to board Perry's ship secretly and search for information that would reveal the intentions of the foreign barbarians. To this day, the Sawamura family archives in Mie Prefecture's Iga-Ueno City still contain the two documents purloined by their stealthy ancestor—two letters containing a

Dutch sailor song extolling the delights of French women in bed and British women in the kitchen.

NINJUTSU IN THE MODERN WORLD

As Japan emerged from the devastation of World War II, all martial arts were banned from practice for a time by the American occupation forces that ruled the conquered nation. Ninjutsu came to be seen as a pointless antique by the Japanese people themselves as they adjusted to a role of international cooperation in the postwar era. Along with the introduction of Western troops, culture, and political concepts into Japan came a reliance on skill in commerce and economics to provide for the security and general welfare of the people. The Japanese of today belongs to the corporation instead of the clan; his armor has been replaced by the ubiquitous dark-blue suit; and his *monsho* (family crest) has become the company lapel pin. Training in the skills of survival no longer takes place in the mountains. In glass and steel skyscrapers, a new kind of knowledge is taught for a new kind of competition on the commercial battlefields of today.

Finding a master of the dark art of ninjutsu in modern westernized Japan seems as unlikely as finding an active practitioner of the magic of Merlin in contemporary industrialized England. Yet, incredibly enough, the art did survive through centuries of obscurity. The ways of the ninja were secretly perpetuated by a small group of quiet, concerned men, committed to the ideals of enlightenment set forth by their ancestors. In the mountain forests of Iga the knowledge survived down through the centuries, passed from the Togakure clan to the Toda family, then handed on to Toshitsugu Takamatsu. The young Toshitsugu was trained in what had been northern Iga by Togakure-ryu ninja of the Toda family, and later earned the name Mongolian Tiger while living and studying with the best of the boxing masters in China during the early 1900s. Master Takamatsu kept his ninja training a secret throughout his entire life. So thorough was the deception that when his neighbors read of his background in the obituaries in 1972, they were stunned.

Toshitsugu Takamatsu, having inherited the legacy of the To-gakure-ryu, willed it on to its thirty-fourth generation in Masaaki Hatsumi, who in the 1950s and 1960s traveled across Japan every week to study with his teacher. Now in middle age and an osteo-path by profession, Masaaki Hatsumi passes on the knowledge of the centuries from his quiet small-town residence in Noda City, a little north of Tokyo.

2 ✦ *SEARCH FOR THE NINJA*

I arrived in Noda City, Chiba Prefecture, on a warm June evening in 1975. It had not been easy finding the place, its small railroad depot now busy with commuters hurrying home for supper. Gnomelike farm women tottered out, bent under massive crates of vegetables tied to their backs. A group of schoolgirls in dour blue uniforms spotted the foreigner and tittered behind hands raised to their mouths. Wearily, knowing no one, I looked about the tiny train station and asked in rather shaky Japanese how to get to the hotel. There was polite laughter, as such towns have only *ryokan* (small, old-fashioned inns) for travelers. A phone call was made for me, and someone kindly allowed me to ride along to the inn.

Many years of reading about the ninja had brought me to this small town on the Edo River. To pursue my interest I had crossed the sea from America to Iga, ancient home of the ninja, only to find that the only ninjutsu left there was a few tattered black suits, swords, and scrolls locked in museum display-cases. A historian had suggested that I might try seeking a ninja master named Hatsumi, who ran perhaps the last remaining school of ninjutsu, somewhere near Tokyo. Taking trains to catch other trains, I had finally arrived in Noda City to ask if he would accept me in his training program.

At the Atsusa Ryokan, when told there was a call for me, I felt awkward moving down the narrow little hallways to the telephone. I was indeed the first American ever to have stayed at the inn. The tiny landlady scampered down the hall ahead of me and handed me the phone.

"Mr. Hayes?" The voice on the telephone was deep and articulate. "We have been waiting for you. Hatsumi Sensei received your letter."

I had gotten no answer to my letter asking permission to view the ninja training school. When I asked about this, I was told that there had been no need for a reply. Hatsumi Sensei had 'seen" that I would be coming regardless. They simply waited for my arrival.

"I am one of the teachers at the ninja school. Hatsumi Sensei would like to meet you and speak with you. May we visit you this evening?"

The meeting had come a little sooner than I had expected. I hurriedly changed from dusty blue jeans to a suit and tie that I had brought along specifically for the purpose of making a favorable impression on the last master of the ninja tradition. I mentally rehearsed a formal greeting that I had memorized for the occasion.

The darkness surrounding the inn soon produced the two men. The master's assistant appeared first, dressed casually in knit trousers and a golf sweater. We exchanged brief greetings and bows, and then he reached out and shook my hand in Western fashion. He had a warm smile, but he moved with quiet precision and I saw a look of cool, intense appraisal in his eyes. Hatsumi Sensei, the master, followed him into the light with a jaunty, relaxed gait, his hands tucked in the back pockets of off-white jeans. He had short graying hair and wore a maroon polo shirt. He didn't bow, but gave a sort of chopping salute and shook my hand, then motioned us all back into the inn. His manner was casual, almost uninterested.

I later learned that it was most unusual for Hatsumi Sensei to leave his house to visit others. This master of the silent art prefers anonymity. He remains at home, and those who wish to see him must seek him out. This man who was born five hundred years too late leaves his dwelling for walks through the streets and countryside at night, moving with the shadows to perfect his art.

We sat on *tatami* (woven mats) around a low square table, sipping delicately flavored green tea and munching rice crackers. We talked till midnight, the master asking about my life and motivations, my travels, places in which I had lived, things and people I had known.

"How many languages do you speak?"

I wondered what that had to do with ninja training. "Three, sir. English, German, and Japanese." He looked as though he were pleased with my answer.

"You graduated from a university? What did you study there?"

I wished I could tell him that I had studied law, or history, or medicine—something that might have sounded more impressive. "I studied acting and theater direction."

"Ah, very good. These approach the true skills of the ninja. When a man can disguise his true intent, and has the sensitivity to recognize the hidden motives of others, he is capable of becoming a shrewd fighter and a difficult adversary."

I tried to ask Hatsumi Sensei specific questions about the fighting aspects of ninjutsu, and his school's training methods. He would answer briefly and then counter with questions about my interests and background. It was surprising to me that my previous martial arts experience was of little interest to these men. Explanations of my past training in the Oriental self-defense methods, into which I was prepared to go at great length, were noted perfunctorily by the master and his assistant. Personal questions,

37

the answers to which I had never really thought through before, seemed to be much more important to them.

At one point I was describing a difficult *kata* of preset movements that I had learned in order to qualify for my latest black-belt promotion, when the master shocked me by interrupting my discourse with an imitation of the movements of the *kata*. His movements were technically perfect, and yet they somehow looked awkward and out of place. The masters I had seen perform the *kata* series before had made the precise, rigid motions seem dynamic and impressive. The master made them look robot-like and comical. I then realized that the stiff moves did not fit Hatsumi Sensei's relaxed and natural bearing, and the contrast had produced the ludicrous effect. For a man who was constantly rigid and controlled, however, the stylized moves would fit his personality and appear appropriate. The master merely commented that the system I was describing had been a stage through which he, too, had passed in his youth.

Hatsumi Sensei did the little imitation again, and laughed pleasantly with his assistant. I smiled politely, not really knowing how to handle the situation. This master of the ninja was not acting anything like I had thought he would. I had been expecting someone slightly sinister, formal, and reserved. Instead, here he was casually laughing and treating me as though we had been acquaintances for years. I was a little confused and uncomfortable.

He took a sip of tea and asked when I had been born.

"September 9, 1949, by our calendar."

Hatsumi Sensei raised his eyebrows slightly and his mouth turned down at the corners in an odd smile. "Born on the ninth day of the ninth month of the forty-ninth year of the century you call the nineteen hundreds. That is interesting. According to our ancient traditions, nine represents the highest level of personal growth."

I must have looked a little perplexed. The master paused a moment and tried to explain again. "There are nine levels or steps to

15. Masaaki Hatsumi, master of the Togakure-ryu, strikes a fighting pose.

personal development, from base physicality to highest spirituality. The ninja knew how to reach and utilize the power of any level—that is why they were so advanced. They were not supermen. They were merely completely developed natural men. Not all ninja were equally skilled at attaining all nine levels. Each man has his own inherent limitations, you know.''

I nodded as though I knew.

"The first three levels deal with physical development. Our

39

ninja training begins with the first level, or base physicality. The students practice leaping and tumbling, how to hit the ground safely and quietly, and techniques of body conditioning for suppleness and agility. This is the basis for the fundamentals of unarmed defense. The ninja's system of unarmed fighting is called *taijutsu*. It is divided into two subsystems: *daken-taijutsu* [the way of attacking the bones], which is made up of strikes, kicks, and blocks; and *ju-taijutsu* [the relaxed-body method], which is composed of grappling and throwing techniques. Real fighting always involves both elements."

"Like karate and judo combined," I interjected as he paused briefly.

"Well, not exactly." Hatsumi Sensei did not seem to see any relationship between his martial art and the others. As far as he was concerned, I could have been comparing ninjutsu to wine tasting and insect collecting. "You see, karate and judo are taught mostly as sports today. The ninja's *taijutsu* was developed for use in mortal combat. Here, let us show you what we are talking about. Please throw a punch at Tanemura-san."

The master's assistant rose to his feet and moved close to me. He appeared to be in his late twenties and, though not as tall as I, was of solid build. I hesitated for a moment, not knowing how to handle the situation. The man stood there in a relaxed manner. What should I do? Should I really try to hit him? I waited for him to get ready.

"Please. Throw a punch at Tanemura-san." He was just standing there when I finally let loose a right-hand punch that ripped through the air toward his face.

He moved as effortlessly as a curtain in the wind to the inside of my punch, letting my fist sail through the empty space where his face had been. Flipping his left fist up and across, he struck my punching hand beneath the thumb. It was over in half a second. He had punched my punch and my whole arm felt as though it had turned to ice. The tingling, frozen feeling extended from armpit to fingertips; my hand hung limp, incapable of opening. I must have looked absolutely pitiful, for both men laughed and shook their heads.

Hatsumi Sensei was right. It wasn't like the karate I had practiced for over eight years. I grinned weakly and sat down at the table again. The master's assistant continued to stand.

"That was *daken-taijutsu*, the striking method. Now we would like to show you how *ju-taijutsu*, the grappling method, is different from judo. Please grab the front of Tanemura-san's jacket and slam him against the wall."

My hand and arm had not yet regained feeling, and I was supposed to attack this man again? Reluctantly, I stood and gingerly took the fabric of his jacket in my left hand. I held my breath in anticipation of the coming fury.

16. Hatsumi Sensei overcomes multiple assailants.

17. Hatsumi Sensei applies a sword technique.

The master smiled broadly. He was thoroughly enjoying the scene. "That wasn't much of an attack. Go ahead! Really grab him and move him!"

I looked down at the man. He looked so peaceful standing there in front of me. The wall was about 4 feet behind him. I tightened my grip on his jacket and started to shove into his chest. His arms flew up and over mine, and then he got some sort of hold on my wrist and elbow. I didn't even have time to scream. The pain roared up my arm and I fell to the floor in a heap, to be pinned there looking at his stockinged foot. Curiously, I could see only his right foot. As his grip relaxed and I looked up, I noticed that his left knee was poised in the air to strike. As I crawled to my feet, the master commented, "In a real fight, one would knock the adversary out by bringing the knee up into his jaw as he dropped to the ground. It is interesting, isn't it."

I nodded dully. It had been more a statement than a question anyway. The master filled my teacup as I took my seat. I didn't trust either of my hands yet, so I let the tea cool for a moment on the table.

Hatsumi Sensei went on to explain that the first level of training also includes the use of various weapons. The ninja's arsenal is quite extensive. He must learn to fight with stick and staff weapons, swords and knives, chains, anything that might be used against him or that he might be able to pick up in a combat situation. Techniques of invisible movement and other basic physical skills are also taught.

The second level is concerned with the generation and channeling of the body's energies. There are various types of energy: creative, physical, emotional, and so on. These energies stem from different centers in the body and are revealed in different aspects of the personality. The ninja must be able to tap the energy source appropriate for what he wants to do. If he is too tense, he must calm himself. If he faces grave danger, he must rouse himself up. If he feels that someone is manipulating him, he must augment his sensitivity and awareness. This is possible through control of the subtle aspects of the body's physicality.

In the third phase of development, the ninja learns to use the dynamic force of the universe. The West does not acknowledge anything like this force. The Orient sees it in everything living as well as static. The trick is to learn how to tune into this natural force and make it work for one. Natural body movement eventually replaces conventional muscle power in fighting, whether one is punching or slashing with a sword. In this way, even an old and seemingly weak ninja is still capable of exercising great power. In fact, the older he gets, the stronger he gets.

When the master had finished, Tanemura-san stood and said, "Allow me to show you how this force works. Please stand."

With great apprehension, I took my feet gain. "Please position your body so that I will not be able to knock you over if I push you," he instructed.

I settled into a solid pose and looked at Tanemura-san. He moved toward me slowly and raised his hand until the palm was aimed at my upper chest. The hand suddenly darted toward my chest. I braced for the impact, but there was none. The hand stopped about 4 inches from me, but I had already begun to pitch forward in anticipation of the blow. I tried to pull back, and as a result toppled backward. The man hadn't even touched me, yet I had to brace my hand on the wall to keep from falling. I felt a bit foolish, and could only smile and shake my head.

"In America we call that a 'psych-out,' " I laughed. "You get your opponent to believe you will do something that you don't really intend to do."

The master opened his eyes wide and asked in a tone of sincere concern, "You mean that you really couldn't feel the force of the blow?"

I was unsure of what to say. I felt that he was having fun at my expense. Perhaps seeing how gullible I was.

My failure to reply was a clear enough reply for the master. He instructed Tanemura-san to perform the technique once more, a little harder this time.

Tanemura-san positioned himself in front of me again, and cautioned me to brace myself to comfortably accept the force of the blow. He held his right hand lightly in front of his chest, palm out. "I will use the flat surface of my hand, and strike at the muscular portion of your chest for the sake of safety. However, please imagine what it would feel like if I were to strike the bony center of your chest with the bones of my fist." The hand floated in the air about 4 inches from my left lapel. "I would also cover more distance with the strike in a real fight and thus develop more power."

He shifted his body forward and at the same time lowered his hips and straightened his arm, forcing his palm into my chest. There was a slight hissing of exhaled breath. The movement was light, almost casual, and there was no tensing up or forcing through.

I felt as though I had been hit by a cannon ball. The impact of the hand itself did not hurt so much, but the jolt sent me flying backward into the wall. I hit the wooden surface with a thud, my shoulders involuntarily pulling down and inward. The thought flashed through my mind that the innkeeper would be worried at all the noise, and then I suddenly realized that I could not breathe. Tanemura-san had not hit me in any obvious vital spot, and yet I felt dizzy and extremely tired, completely drained.

I tottered forward and took my seat, trying to appear as normal and nonchalant as possible. I had a feeling of creeping apprehension about these men. I didn't know how far to trust them, and yet I would have given anything to possess their skills and knowledge.

"Are you all right?" Hatsumi Sensei asked.

"Oh, sure. Just fine," I croaked, still unable to breathe.

"You must be quite strong," the master commented blandly. "That demonstration would have knocked the wind out of most people." He wasn't looking at me when he spoke; I thought he was trying not to laugh.

He explained that beyond the three levels of physical training lie three more dealing with mental development, and then three final steps for spiritual growth, or what is called psychic ability today. The mental and spiritual levels teach the ninja how to heal himself and others through medicine, diet, and balance, and how to fit in with the forces of nature. He learns to study his own mind to gain understanding of others, and ways of sharpening his sensitivity to the finer vibrations in the environment. "Can you imagine fighting a man who could read your mind?" the master asked. "If you wanted to hit him with a chair, his foot would already be on top of the chair. If you tried to punch him, he would already be behind you. If you wanted to shoot him, his knife would have already flown across the room into your chest. If you plotted his demise, he simply would not show up. A very difficult adversary, eh?"

"Have you ever considered writing a book about the training?" I asked.

Tanemura-san spoke. "Hatsumi Sensei has written several books in Japanese. Some deal with philosophy, and others are for children."

"Do they explain any of the techniques, or the higher powers of the ninja? Or how to develop these abilities?"

Hatsumi Sensei looked at me curiously. "No, of course not. This knowledge is not for the public. In any case, no one would believe in these abilities unless he had seen them in action." He handed me a copy of one of his children's books. It was illustrated with pictures of skulking figures in black outfits that resembled jumpsuits. They were engaged in various types of combat with an incredible assortment of weapons. "This is what the public thinks ninjutsu is, so we humor it. The real secrets that have been handed down through the generations are not for publication. They are for the knowledge of a chosen few.

"Americans have visited our training hall, but we have never taught them the true techniques of our system. We have never let an American stay and study with us. Unfortunately, our art is greatly misunderstood today, and the ninja legends tend to attract the kind of people whom we do not feel it wise to teach. Even a Japanese must have references to speak on his behalf in order to gain entrance to our hall. We are looking for the rare individual who has the ability and desire to combine the strengths of both the fierce warrior and the benevolent sage in one personality. We have no time for the idly curious, the mentally or emotionally unstable, or those merely seeking thrills or personal glory."

It sounded like a roundabout way of dismissing me. I had to hide my heartbreak. After the long journey here and this remarkable meeting, the knowledge of the ninja was just as elusive as ever. This last great possibility was slipping through my grasp.

"Well, it was a privilege to at least meet you, sir. I really appreciate your taking the time to speak with me tonight." I bowed to the ninja before they slipped away, back into the night.

"Oh, you will see me again. Perhaps this is the time to make our training a little more open to other peoples of the world, since you have come all this way seeking us. In a broader view of reality that many people would not want to understand, you have been on your way here for longer than you perhaps realize. Tanemura-san will come to pick you up tomorrow night at 9 o'clock, and you will have your first ninjutsu lesson with him then." Hatsumi Sensei smiled in a reassuring way that seemed to contradict his startling words, further confusing my attempts to understand his motivations and logic. "We will accept you for training in our dojo, if that is what you want. And for tonight, do sleep well."

47

3 ✦ *UNARMED COMBAT*

Insects chirped somewhere in the darkness. Distant bullfrogs croaked. On a windless night of little moon, I looked out over acres of shallow water, out of which rice plants poked tentatively.

I stood next to my teacher in the night of Japan's rural Saitama Prefecture, half a world away from my American birthplace. We were clad in black cotton jackets, loose-fitting black leggings, and black *tabi* (split-toed footwear). My teacher's tattered sash was embroidered with the Japanese characters 戸隠流忍法 for Togakure-ryu Nimpo, the Togakure family school of the art of stealth.

My first training session was to deal with unarmed combat. Tanemura-san had arrived at the inn as promised and we had driven through the darkness to his home in the country. He stressed again that there were two aspects to real fighting—striking and grappling. Our training would blend both elements.

THE NINJA FISTS

In the darkness of that night my initiation into the way of the ninja began. Tanemura-san, now my teacher, asked me to demonstrate some punching techniques. I slammed my right fist

18. Unarmed combat training.

straight out in front of my body, while snapping my left fist back to my left hip. I knew that he would be impressed by this punch that could smash through three planks of wood.

"Well, that is a rather old-fashioned punching technique. It was devised by the Okinawan farmers hundreds of years ago to combat the armored samurai who dominated them. I do not think it is very reliable against today's fighters. I'm afraid that they are much faster today since they usually wear no armor." The samurai of old were clad in bamboo and leather armor. Naturally, this slightly slowed their movements. Therefore, the Okinawan farmer could afford to concentrate on delivering single blows with enough power to smash through the adversary's armor.

"What does the ninja's punching method look like?" I asked.

"There is no one punching method. The hand can be formed into many different positions. The experienced fighter uses his hand in whatever way it can best be used. Different targets of the body should be attacked by appropriate striking surfaces of the hand. Here are a few of the ninja fists."

49

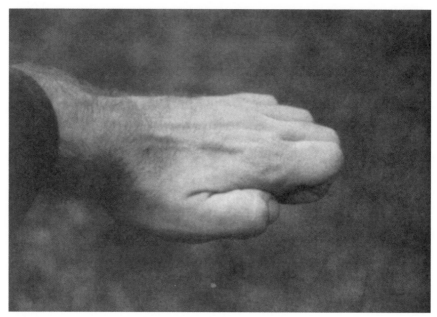

19. Shikan-ken.

Shikan-ken (Extended-Knuckle Fist)

Tanemura-san explained that the *shikan-ken* is the fundamental fist of the Togakure-ryu. It is used against hard, broad surfaces of bone structure. The fist is formed with the fingers half-folded, leaving the middle knuckles protruding. The striking points are the knuckles, which may be applied to the facial bones, breastbone, and sides of the middle ribs.

The punch goes straight in, bullet-like, with all of the force behind the striking points. The elbow should not rise along the outside of the fist's path, or the punch will bend and hook. The elbow is kept close to the ribs, forcing the punch straight into the target. The teacher warned that the fist is not flipped into place

50

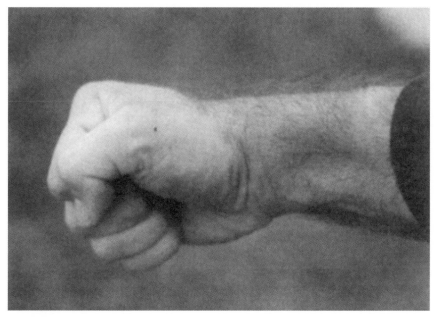

20. Fudo-ken.

and withdrawn, but used to knock the adversary back. The thrust of the punch continues through the impact with the target.

Fudo-ken (Clenched Fist)

This is the conventional clenched fist, which can be used to strike from many different angles. It is used against a variety of targets, but is especially effective against areas of the body in which the edges of the bone structure are accessible. This fist is formed by curling the fingers into the palm and clamping the thumb beside the index finger. The front slab of the fist, the outside knuckles, or the inside knuckles can be used to strike targets such as the nose, jaw, lower edges of the ribs, arms, and legs.

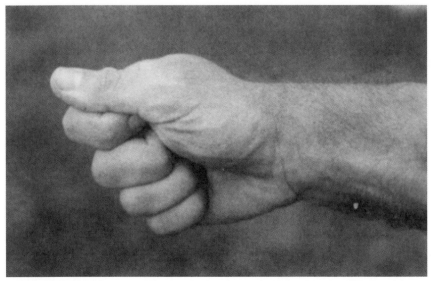

21. Boshi-ken.

Boshi-ken (Thumb-Drive Fist)

The *boshi-ken* is unique to the ninja's system of combat. This fist's single striking point is used against semisoft targets, generally muscles covering bone structure. It is especially well suited for attacking nerve centers with precision. The fist is formed with the thumb protruding, and the hand in a position resembling that used to grip a golf club. The thumb is positioned for a driving jab, reinforced by the curled index finger. This single striking point is used to attack targets such as the side of the neck, the sides of the upper ribs, the solar plexus, and the lower abdomen to the inside of the hip bones. As with most of the punches in ninjutsu, it is essential to follow powerfully through the target, and not merely poke and retreat.

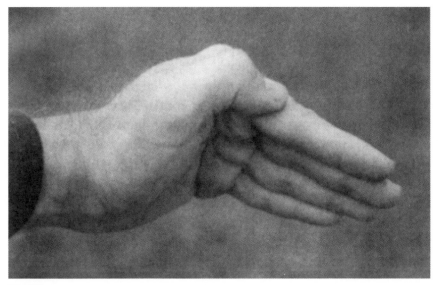

22. Shuto.

Shuto (Sword Hand)

The sword hand is not really a fist, but it is an important striking weapon. The lower outside edge of the palm is used against the structures of the limbs and neck, as well as for striking into the joints. In the *shuto*, the planes of the palm and fingers form an angle of 45 degrees, and the thumb is clamped along the base of the index finger.

When beginning the sword-hand strike, maintain the hand in a conventional fist to disguise your intention. The hand swings around into the target, drawing power from the weight and motion of the arm and body. At the instant before contact, the hand is opened to *shuto* position and smashed through the target at a 90-degree angle to its surface. The hand is not flicked into place and quickly withdrawn. The strike is intended to stun or to break through the bone structure attacked.

FIGHTING POSTURES

Tanemura-san then asked me to assume my usual fighting position so that we could practice the strikes. I was pleased that he had the foresight to build upon the knowledge that I already had. As I had been a practitioner of the martial arts for years, there was no point in wasting time going over such things as how to stand. I assumed the fighting stance with my right side to the teacher, my fists at my side ready to block or strike, and my legs in position as though I were riding an invisible horse. A little bouncing motion added unpredictability to the pose.

The teacher cocked his head and frowned. "Very dangerous, I think. Watch this." He began a move toward me. I immediately tried to hop back, but found myself pinned in place by the pressure of his foot against the side of my knee. The pain built and I was forced to a sitting position on the ground. "In a true fight, the move would be executed quickly, injuring the knee before knocking the adversary down."

I was a little annoyed. I hadn't expected him to go for my leg. I was used to practicing killing and knockout techniques, not tripping people up. What use could there be in leg attacks?

"Please stand." The teacher released my leg and the pain began to disappear. "You must be ready to protect the legs. If your leg is injured, you cannot stand or move about properly. You will lose the fight or be killed.

"Naturally, in a sport such as kendo or kickboxing there are rules and limitations for safety, and body positions can be used that would otherwise be dangerous. By the same token, the conventional boxer does not worry about foot sweeps, and the practitioner of judo does not concern himself with finger jabs to the eyes. Ninjutsu, however, is intended for actual combat. Perhaps I should show you a few of the ninja's fighting postures."

Kamae (body posture) in its essence is best understood as the physical embodiment of mental attitude. Or, even simpler, body positioning should be appropriate for what the fighter is doing at any given moment. Unlike some martial arts, the ninja's *taijutsu* does not utilize fixed or rigid stances or foot positions. The *kamae* of *taijutsu* are loosely held, with the fighter moving briefly in and out of the various postures. Postures are assumed as fighting movements are performed, in a natural and spontaneous flow.

The Togakure ninja's choice of fighting posture is determined by his relationship to his adversary. This represents an application of the philosophical view that everything is a result and cause of other things, and indeed the reality of anything is based on its relationships to these others. There is no completely independent or isolated object in existence—everything is inescapably entwined. Therefore the fighter must constantly adapt to the changing variety of circumstances that constitutes each unique moment of existence.

The ninja interprets the interrelationships of the world through the framework of five ways in which things are manifested. The first manifestation, the void, is the basis of the four physical manifestations, which descend from the void in order from the most ethereal to the most solid. The four fighting postures are based on the physical manifestations.

空 *Ku* (void): subatomic energy; the "nothing" from which all things take their form
風 *Fu* (wind): things in a gaseous state; receiving posture
火 *Ka* (fire): things in an energy-releasing state; offensive posture
水 *Sui* (water): things in a liquid state; defensive posture
地 *Chi* (earth): things in a solid state; natural posture

Shizen no Kamae (Natural Posture)

Tanemura-san said, "The *shizen no kamae* is the first fighting position, and it is most important. You should become completely familiar with this pose, and thoroughly understand its value, as it is used to handle almost all surprise attacks."

23. Shizen no kamae.

I waited for the teacher to assume the fighting pose, but he didn't move. He continued to stand in front of me with his feet in normal position about hip-width apart, each leg supporting an equal amount of weight. His arms hung loosely at his sides with hands relaxed and open, and his gaze was leveled at me.

Long seconds of silence passed, and the teacher spoke again. "Please assume the natural fighting posture so that we can continue the lesson." He was still looking right at me.

I was a little surprised. "That's the fighting stance? Just standing there?"

"Of course. If a man is intent on harming or killing you, he is not likely to inform you first. You must begin to protect yourself from the second you perceive his intentions. You will usually be standing or walking in such a pose as this."

The natural posture reflects the solidity of the earth, and the fighting techniques employed from this pose make use of a stable, grounded feeling. The body weight and, to some degree, the consciousness are centered in the hips at the bottom tip of the spine. The legs are relaxed and yet firmly in touch with the ground, as though they were the subterranean roots of a mountain or a half-buried boulder. The knees are straight, not locked back or bent forward, and the muscles are maintained in a comfortable, flexed state.

The teacher instructed me to punch him in the face. I stepped forward and swung my right arm in a relaxed looping punch to his jaw. He held his ground and batted the inside of my forearm with his right hand, sending my arm flying backward with the jolt and throwing me off balance. I felt as though I had just slammed my forearm into a tree trunk.

Tanemura-san's face had a slightly annoyed look to it. "You do not need to go halfway with me. To experience the techniques properly, you must fully apply them. Please throw a real punch that I cannot knock away."

I shook some feeling back into my arm and then launched my right fist straight at the teacher's face. I was punching at full speed, but it seemed as though I were moving in slow motion. My punch was only half-unfolded when the teacher's fist sailed into my face. Fortunately for me, he choked back on his punch at the last moment to cushion the impact.

He had lowered his hips, turning them to his left while angling his left foot slightly inward to accommodate the body twist. His left arm had shot straight up and forward along the inside of my punching arm. Though he was smaller than me, he could out-reach me in this position because his left shoulder was turned and extended with the punch. He appeared to be unstable, but I was unable to unbalance him when invited to try to shove him over. It was like trying to knock over a fire hydrant.

The *shizen no kamae* and its earth-power principle were next demonstrated as a defense against a wrestling attack. I was invited to try to throw the teacher to the ground in any way I chose. I was even allowed to get a secure grip on him.

I had decided to use our size difference to my advantage, by knocking his shoulders backward while sweeping his leg forward with my own. The teacher countered my attack merely by slightly lowering his hips, and again I felt as though I were facing an immovable object. His back remained straight and he hadn't even tensed his muscles, yet despite my weight advantage I was still maddeningly unable to budge him.

The teacher's right hand had ended up resting on my left shoulder during the struggle, and I hadn't really noticed it. Suddenly the fingers curled inward, sliding behind my left collarbone at the base of my neck. As his fingertips drove down, his thumb pushed up on the bottom of the narrow bone. There was no great power exerted, but the effect was phenomenal. I caught my breath with a gasp and my hands flew up in an attempt to relieve the excruciating pain. As my body involuntarily jerked upward, it was easy for the teacher to slam me straight down to the ground.

I sat there rubbing my chest, amazed at what had just happened. The teacher was still standing where he had been before we began, as though he were a tree rooted to the spot. He didn't show any sign of having been in a struggle. He commented in an emotionless, almost bored voice, "You should have kept your hips lower when you tried the throw. Always remember, when your fighting techniques seem to lack power, it means that you are not close enough to the ground."

24. Ichimonji no kamae.

Ichimonji no Kamae (Defensive Posture)

I next studied the defensive posture, which is used to counter the attacker's techniques. The *ichimonji no kamae* reflects the fluidity of water, and the fighting techniques employed from this pose make use of a flexible, elusive feeling. The body weight is centered in the abdomen, behind and below the navel. The torso is angled sideways toward the adversary, and the back is straight with the rear leg supporting most of the weight.

59

Tanemura-san assumed the posture by shifting his hips down and away from me, as though he were going to sit in an invisible chair. His rear foot moved back quickly, and his front foot was dragged into place so that it pointed at me, the two feet forming the letter L. His hips were low on deeply sprung legs. His leading hand floated at the end of an extended arm, and his rear hand was in position next to his cheek with the elbow protecting his ribs.

As I tried to grab the teacher to throw him, he evaded me by shifting and angling inside and outside my arms. When I tried to catch his leading hand, he simply let it roll with my grasp and into my eye. No matter how far I reached or how quickly I moved, his body was always 3 inches out of reach.

I finally lashed out with a long right front kick that I thought would have to catch him. Instead of backing up, he cut to his right and inside my kicking leg. Hopping onto his right leg, he lifted his leading left leg in an outward crescent-like swing. The outside edge of his foot caught my kicking leg in the middle of the calf, quickly and easily kicking my kick out of the air and bringing my leg to the ground.

As I lurched onto my crumbling right leg, it seemed natural to use my lunging body motion to throw a right punch. In response the teacher continued to cut to his right, leading me around in a circle. He always maintained the defensive posture, moving with the rear foot while dragging the leading leg into position so that it was aimed right at me. As my right fist sailed into the space where his head had been, he looped his left fist up and into the underside of my wrist. He had no sooner made impact than he shifted his hips to his left and brought the edge of his open right hand smashing down onto my right forearm. My arm felt as though it had been hit with a shotgun blast. I completely forgot about the fight and clutched my battered arm, fearing that it had been permanently damaged.

"Your arm is all right, though it will be about 15 seconds before you will be able to make a fist again. The important thing to remember about the defensive posture is to move your hips first and let your body follow. Do not make the mistake of leading with the shoulders. Likewise, do not rely on foot movement to start a body motion. The shoulder lead results in poor balance and the foot lead is too slow. If you stay low and shift the hips in the direction desired, the feet and shoulders will follow efficiently. It should feel as though somebody were grabbing you by the belt and pulling you into position. That way you can stay just outside the enemy's reach, and yet stay close enough to counterattack immediately after your defense. You can be like the ocean waves, ebbing and then crashing back."

Jumonji no Kamae (Offensive Posture)

Once the principles of defense have been internalized, the student of ninjutsu progresses to the offensive posture, in which he moves forward to meet his adversary. The fists are positioned in front of the chin, crossed at the wrists and ready to strike or to block an incoming attack. The elbows are held low over the ribs for protection, and the hand of the leading side of the body is in front of the trailing hand. The feet are spaced slightly farther apart than the hips, with one foot leading slightly.

The teacher and I assumed the offensive posture and began some shadow-boxing movements in the moonlight. It was difficult to generate power while keeping my balance on the wet, slippery ground. The teacher called out, "Center your weight lower in your body. Power comes from the trunk, not the shoulders. If you rely on your shoulders, you can be thrown easily, and your punches will never be powerful enough to injure an attacker larger than yourself."

The offensive posture reflects the intensity of fire, and the fighting techniques employed from this position make use of a determined, resolute feeling. The body weight and the consciousness are centered behind the solar plexus, at the bottom of the breastbone. As with the other fighting postures, the back is held

61

25. Jumonji no kamae.

straight and the body never leans beyond the range of the feet. To move in the offensive posture, the leading foot slides forward with the toes at a slight inward angle. The knees stay flexed to keep the center of gravity low and stable, and to facilitate quick movement.

Again Tanemura-san and I took positions across from each other. I settled into the offensive posture and waited to see what he would do. The teacher looked at me and commented, "You should not be in the offensive posture if you do not intend to attack. It is dangerous to assume a body posture that does not conform to your intention.''

As I contemplated his words, the teacher rushed at me in a sudden attack. His movements had an incredible simultaneity to them. He was not throwing a punch and following with his body, nor moving close and then punching—his fists, shoulders, and hips all came forward in the same motion. He moved as quickly and steadily as though pulled by a rope attached to the front of his jacket.

The logic in his previous comment quickly became evident. I had been standing in the offensive posture somewhat absent-mindedly, and suddenly found myself in need of a defense. In the next few seconds, I was so busy dealing with my own body that I had no way of handling my attacker. His leading hand flew out in a straight punch to the underside of my right forearm, which I was holding up in a defensive covering action. Then, before I could even move the aching limb, the teacher swung his trailing fist around and down onto the back of my right hand, using the inside knuckles of his fist as if knocking on a door. This lightning one-two combination was immediately applied to my other arm as well, as the teacher drove ever forward.

My battered arms were swept away and I felt knuckles drilling in between my ribs. My right hand was seized in a vicelike grip and the arm twisted back. The arm turned to its limit, and then the pain forced me off my feet. I landed on my back only to be pinned to the ground.

I was soon on my feet again and ready for another demonstration of the fierce intensity of the offensive posture. This time I was alert, ready to defend myself. Tanemura-san executed a sort of jab with his right hand and then, leading with his left side, delivered a long, straight, driving punch with his left fist. As the fist approached my face, I moved my right arm up to knock the punch away. The teacher had known that I would block his punch, and as his fist slid over my blocking arm he snapped the

26(a), (b). Practicing the heel stamp.

hand open and brought its edge cutting down on the perfect target presented by my upraised right forearm. The painful blow knocked my right arm completely out of the way, but as it flew back I found my left hand grabbing the teacher's right sleeve cuff.

He was now too close to kick me, and I wasn't letting him get away . . . yet somehow I felt his heel sinking into my midsection. He had pulled his knee up high in the narrow space between us, aimed his heel at me, and straightened his leg. I tried to brace myself, but it was too late—onto my seat again, looking up.

The heel stamp is used at close range. The impact can injure, and the body motion behind the kick should knock the adversary back. The toes are curled back and the heel is shoved into the adversary, as though kicking in a locked door. A low hip position in the offensive posture assures the kick will have stability and power.

Hira no Kamae (Receiving Posture)

The fourth fighting pose we practiced was the *hira no kamae*. The teacher spread his feet slightly and flexed his knees a bit. He raised his arms just above his shoulders and held them out to the sides with the palms forward. He looked like he was about to hug somebody, and I wondered how that unlikely looking pose could be used in combat.

When instructed to charge, I felt a little silly attacking a spread-eagled victim, but nonetheless moved in with a right punch to the ribs and a left to the face. As my initial right punch approached Tanemura-san's midsection, he pivoted to his right on his left foot like a puppet suspended on strings, floating back and to the outside of my right arm. His arms remained outstretched as he seized my right wrist with his right hand and slapped my right ear with his open left hand. Distracted by the ringing in my head, I was quickly wedged into an elbow-bar arm lock and forced to the ground.

The receiving posture reflects the lightness of the air, and the fighting techniques employed from this pose make use of an evasive, whirlwind feeling. The body weight and the consciousness are centered in the chest at a point behind the middle of the breastbone, and as this center moves the body follows.

In position to fight again, we moved around each other in intertwining circles. The teacher held the receiving pose and moved by shifting his feet in swirling patterns. He looked like the sail of a ship catching the wind. As my punches flew at him, he ducked and weaved to avoid them. There was a relaxed naturalness about his movement, and unlike a boxer who might bob and weave with head and shoulders only, the ninjutsu teacher allowed his entire body to shift. When I punched at his face, he would duck forward and outside my punching arm, and counter with a swinging thumb-drive to my solar plexus. When I kicked, he would pinwheel his arms to catch my leg from the underside and dump me to the ground.

At one point I executed a low left front kick to his right hip. His hands dropped for defense and he moved to his left to avoid my strike. As he moved, I immediately let loose a right roundhouse kick toward the left side of his head. My height would allow the kick to sail over his shoulder with ease, and his hands were in a low blocking position to counter my previous technique. There was no way for him to block the high kick.

As my right foot approached his left ear, he simply dived sideways to avoid my strike. He jumped out and up to his right, like a fish leaping gracefully out of a stream for a few seconds. At the height of his dive he threw his arms out to his sides and cartwheeled twice like a human windmill. And there he stood, once more in the receiving posture, out to my left.

As I crossed the rough ground to go after him, two soft slapping sounds came from the front of my jacket, and then I was aware of a slight stinging sensation across my upper abdomen. I looked down to see two pieces of tree bark tumbling down my jacket to the ground.

27. Hira no kamae.

Across from me, the teacher called out, "In a real fight I would have picked up rocks during the handspring, instead of soft old wood." I looked at the ground he had crossed, and noticed that he had directed his cartwheel so that it took him over the one spot in the area where the weeds cleared to reveal jagged debris.

OTHER FACTORS

The ninja engages in unarmed combat for one reason alone—to protect himself or those for whom he is responsible, in situations of mortal danger. Therefore, *taijutsu* aims at inflicting the most damage possible with the fewest and simplest moves possible.

67

The ninja must be ready to meet any adversary and to adopt whatever method will guarentee his survival.

I came to realize that the techniques practiced in the Togakure-ryu training hall number in the thousands. Endless combinations are drilled so that the students will be able to handle any real situation they may face. Obviously, no amount of memorization would be sufficient to cover all the possibilities of real combat; therefore, the fundamentals are taught as responses to broad categories of attack. The appropriate follow-up must be chosen in view of the adversary's attempts at countering action. However, it is possible to pick out a few general factors of particular significance.

Ma-ai (distancing) is of great importance to the clever fighter. The ninja does not stay close to a man who is skilled at infighting. On the other hand, he crowds the man who requires distance for his techniques. The ninja avoids specializing in any one set of techniques that would limit his own range and therefore his effectiveness.

Angling is also of importance in the ninja's fighting method. By moving in an unexpected direction, the fighter can gain the advantage of strategic placement. This frees him from the rather primitive pattern of holding his ground and trying to overpower the adversary with blocks, so that an attack can be launched in a more considered and effective manner.

Perhaps the most important guideline in the Togakure-ryu method of unarmed fighting is the emphasis placed on naturalness, and the ability to fit the defensive situation appropriately. Strength is used when strength will conquer. Evasiveness is used when it will succeed. Speed and power are used when they will overcome. The attacker's momentum is captured when that will bring his defeat. The ninja doesn't look like a man in a fight when he is fighting: he simply moves as appropriate, his body a servant of the strength of his intentions.

4 ✦ WEAPONRY

CHAINS AND CORDS

Hatsumi Sensei held the *kyoketsu-shogei* loosely coiled in his left hand. He moved to a corner of the training hall opposite me, leisurely swinging the ringed end of the cord in his right hand. The narrow cord was approximately 12 feet in length, strong and and resilient. To one end of the cord was fastened a steel ring, which could be tossed over the ends of roof beams, tree limbs, or suitable hooks to form an anchor for climbing the rope. The other end of the cord was attached to a unique hand-held blade. From the wooden handle protruded two edged spikes of steel, at right angles to each other.

I held a defensive position as Hatumi Sensei circled me and lectured the class. He twirled the ringed end of the cord in a small loop and explained how the ring could be used to snag the adversary or knock him unconscious. The master jerked the cord and ring back into his grip. He continued his teaching: Let the ring fly as a natural extension of the swing. Do not deliberately throw it.

The ring left his grip once again. The cord went out to the master's right and snaked its way to the left of my head in a broad arc. This time the master did not pull back. As the ring came within reach, I threw my left hand up and snatched the ring from the air.

Upon catching the ring, I felt a rush of excitement and pride. I had foiled the attack of the master of the ninja. As suddenly as the feeling had come, it was replaced by a feeling of regret. I was deeply embarrassed for the master. His weapon had been so easily intercepted by an inexperienced student from America. I wished that I had not made the catch, and had not made him look foolish in front of his students. I felt that I should have been more thoughtful, more considerate of his rank and position. This feeling, too, was in turn replaced by another. I was suddenly very disappointed that I had been able to catch the weapon so easily. This man was supposed to be the supreme master of the last ninja school in Japan, and I had outmaneuvered him. If he really was the teacher I had hoped he would be, this couldn't have happened. I felt annoyed and let down.

Hatsumi Sensei held his position for the second or two that it took these thoughts to cross my mind. He was about 10 feet away, holding the other end of the cord, looking at me. His expression hadn't changed. He continued to lecture, though I still held the ring firmly. He spoke briefly about "the unexpected." I thought he meant my catching his weapon. He didn't mean that at all.

Hatsumi Sensei snapped his arm up and down briskly, and sent some sort of loop over my clenched left hand. He yanked on the cord and I felt a knotted coil dig into my wrist. He had somehow tied up my arm from across the room. Now I was the one facing the unexpected as I flew across the floor, helplessly lassoed. The master made a slashing move with the blade as I floundered toward him, and commented that the adversary would be easy to finish off in such a situation.

I was stunned; the rest of the class was amused. They shook their heads and laughed out loud. Everybody falls for that setup,

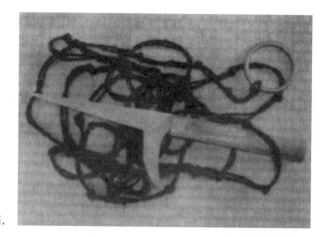

28. Kyoketsu-shogei.

29. Hatsumi Sensei snares an attacker with the kyoketsu-shogei.

30. Kusari-fundo.

31. Gripping the kusari-fundo for concealment.

they told me. It's so easy for Hatsumi Sensei and it always works. The master was smiling as if to say, of course it was a trick. You never know what's coming next. That's what makes this ninjutsu.

Ropes, cords, and chains were favorite weapons of the ninja. These weapons had a long range, were easily compacted and concealed, and could share duties as climbing aids or binding for a captured enemy.

The *kyoketsu-shogei* was used exclusively by ninja. It consists of a dagger blade with a secondary blade hooking out at the hilt, to which is attached a resilient cord from 9 to 12 feet in length. To the end of this cord, made of women's hair in ancient times, is fastened a steel ring 4 inches in diameter.

The *kusari-fundo* is a short length of chain with a steel weight attached to one or both ends. The length of this weapon varies but is usually between 2 and 3 feet. This multipurpose weapon is said to have been invented as a way of countering long-sword techniques without resorting to another sword. It can be constructed easily and is simple to conceal.

32. Gripping the kusari-fundo for combat.

33. Controlling an assailant with the kusari-fundo.

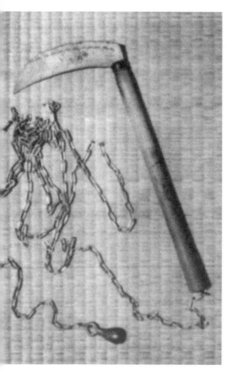

34. Kusari-gama.   35. Gripping the kusari-gama for combat.

The *kusari-gama* is made up of a single-edged blade mounted perpendicularly to a wooden handle, to which a fine chain of 9 to 12 feet is attached. At the end of this chain is a weight of iron, which weighs about the same as the entire chain. Originally developed by farmers, the *kusari-gama* later became a standard fighting tool for samurai as well as ninja.

The *kaginawa* was carried by the ninja primarily to aid in climbing, but also had important uses in close combat with an enemy. It consists of a rope about 30 feet in length attached to a grappling iron with from one to four hooks projecting from it.

74

36. Using the kusari-gama against an attacker.

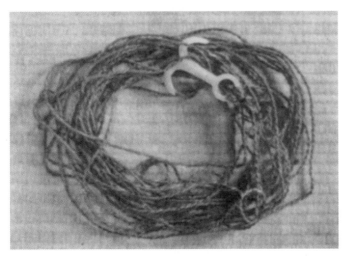

37. Kaginawa.

38. Using the kaginawa for climbing.

The chain or cord is not simply whirled about the body in random circling motions, with the hope of striking whatever comes into range. The weapon is used like a whip, with the striking power concentrated in the tip. Just as in punching or kicking, there is a precise moment and place of impact, on which the ninja must concentrate with deadly accuracy.

When utilizing weapons, it is crucial to maintain effective footwork. The ninja does not stand rooted to the spot, waiting for his adversary to come into proper range. Predictability is avoided by moving with erratic leaps and slides. While executing figure-eight loops or quick slashes and strikes with the weapon, the ninja may choose to move in on his enemy or circle around him, constantly altering and adjusting the distance.

The cord or chain is gripped with the small, ring, and middle fingers. The thumb and index finger are then free to reinforce the grip, or hold the weapon gathered in a wad or loop. This grip method is flexible enough to be used whether striking with the weapon, or using the cord or chain to tangle and ensnare an adversary as he makes an attack.

STICKS AND STAFFS

Each student had been assigned a particular role for the upcoming annual police martial-arts demonstration. We would be showing an entertainingly exaggerated version of the ninja's fighting art to members of the Tokyo Metropolitan Police Department and the reporters that would be covering the event. Each of us had been given a costume and weapons for the show. Tonight's training was to be an acting class, to familiarize us with our roles.

I was to portray a ninja disguised as a wandering monk. Along with prayer beads and other paraphernalia, I had been given a rubber scalp piece to imitate the shaved head of holy men in previous centuries. The shaved head along with my full beard created a rather comical effect, and produced grins and laughter from my fellow students. The dojo radiated a feeling of humor and lively spirits as we settled down together to begin our dramatic training.

In the first scene, a ninja disguised as a crippled beggar was to be set upon by two ruffians. The beggar moved about the training area, supporting himself on a long staff. It was indeed entertaining to watch the student's portrayal of the pitiful character. Wearing a tattered jacket, his head wrapped in a ragged scarf, he gently shifted weight onto his right leg and then quickly stepped with his left while clutching desperately to the staff.

After watching for a few more seconds, I slowly realized that it was not as amusing as I had thought at first. The actor was in reality quite a powerful man who was capable of incredible acrobatics, and was usually springing about the training area on his hands or bouncing up from the floor unexpectedly. Now, however, he seemed to actually feel the pain that mere movement brought to the beggar. It was not a comic exaggeration, but a convincing portrayal of another human being going through life in his own way. The beggar's face had a look of childlike determination to it and, except for an almost imperceptible flash of pain when the weight moved to his right leg, the beggar looked cheerful in his own pathetic way.

His samurai opponents swaggered onto the scene with a brashness that startled me. These actors, in reality polite and sensitive men, callously knocked the beggar out of their way as they moved across the room. It amazed me to see my fellow students in roles so unlike their real personalities. The beggar staggered away painfully, helplessly uttering apologies for being in the way.

The brutal samurai found it offensive that the beggar should speak to them, even in apology, and turned to accost the wretch. The first seized the beggar's coat and drew his hand back to slap the small man. The second smirked and leaned back against a wall to watch the fun.

The beggar's staff came alive. Its tip hit the attacker's wrist to deflect the slap. There was a roar of anger, as though the actor had really felt the pain. The staff continued its work, snaking along the outside of the attacker's right arm, across his chest, and along the left side of his neck. The beggar applied pressure to the samurai's right wrist and his body pinwheeled backward, pivoting on the stationary wooden staff. The samurai hit the floor, his stunned face radiating rage and bewilderment. The scene was as vivid as though it were real, not a mere demonstration.

The second samurai drew a short sword and began hacking at the beggar. The latter used his staff to deflect the sword by striking the samurai's arms and torso as he executed the blows. The beggar hopped and leaped to avoid other slashes. Twice he polevaulted on his staff to a safe part of the training area.

The first attacker was again on his feet with sword drawn. He joined his cohort in a drive to destroy the small man responsible for their humiliation. As they moved in, the beggar's staff came to life again. It whirled with an unearthly hum, speeding to invisibility and seeming to stop in freeze action. Sometimes the staff was a windmill, grinding up arms and legs that got too close. Sometimes it was a whip, lashing out with stinging blows to fragile targets. Sometimes the staff was a battering ram, and sometimes it was a bullet. The actor was in harmony with his weapon, and the staff seemed to be everywhere at the same instant. The attackers were helpless, even though armed with swords.

As the scene drew to a close, the samurai lay on the wooden floor totally incapacitated. The beggar spent a few seconds lovingly dusting off his staff. His eyes seemed to hold a feeling of reverence. He adjusted his tattered scarf, gripped the staff with both hands, and again assumed the beggar's twisted pose. He moved on without looking back at the two men sprawled on the floor.

In Japan's feudal days, sticks and staffs were standard weapons of the culture. Traditional Japanese staff fighting utilized three staffs of varying lengths: the *bo*, 6 feet long; the *jo*, 4 feet long; and the *hambo* (half *bo*), 3 feet long. It is of great importance to contemporary students of ninjutsu that the staff used for practice can be easily replaced by everyday substitutes in the case of actual conflicts. Walking sticks, pool cues, umbrellas, and yard rakes are but a few of the potential weapons that could be picked up and pressed into service if needed.

With all sticks and staffs, the end or tip should be used for striking whenever possible. This is crucial for concentrating the maximum power and speed into the strike. Being hit with a stick is bad enough, but having all the force of the blow concentrated behind a single point vastly increases the leverage and damage potential of the stick as a weapon.

As much as possible, body movement is combined with striking action in the ninja's staff-fighting method. If the hips are coordinated with the staff, additional power will be generated into the strike. This is similar to the principle behind the lunging punch. Body momentum adds to the impact of the striking weapon, whether it be fist or stick.

Obviously, a long staff provides a means of reaching out and

39. The long staff extends the ninja's reach.

attacking adversaries at a distance. However, a clever opponent may be able to judge the length of the staff and position himself just out of range to avoid being hit. Therefore, advantageous use must be made of footwork and staff "travel" in the grip of the hands.

Ninjutsu students first practice basic slashes and poking strikes from a stationary position. Accuracy of movement and delivery to the target are the goals of this training. Next, a forward step with the right foot is added at the same instant the strike is being

40. Subduing an assailant with the short staff.

delivered. For total combat preparedness, the students next practice stepping back with the left foot at the same instant the strike is being delivered. This movement is used when the attacker charges, crowding the ninja using the staff.

The ninjutsu staff-fighting method utilizes one more device or trick: the sliding grip. As the staff arcs around from its ready position to the point of impact, the grip is momentarily loosened. The staff pulls itself through the hands with a forward reaching motion. Just before impact, the grip is tightened again and the tip of the staff is driven into its target with a powerful snap. This centrifugal pull on the swinging staff gives the weapon a seemingly elastic quality. Mastery of this technique demands hours of repetitious training to develop accuracy and timing.

As in unarmed fighting, the most desirable method of dealing with staff attacks is to avoid the need to block. The blocking motion may take just long enough to allow the attacker to execute a follow-up strike. After practicing the fundamental strikes and blocks to build up familiarity and confidence with the stick weapons, the student begins to use the feet to angle and move the body away from attacks. To retreat to the side or back, the rear foot is used to gain ground and pull the body away. To crowd or slip by the attack, the front foot is used to lead the body into or to the side of the attack.

The next step is to develop an ability to counterattack while avoiding the adversary. This could be considered the highest level of staff-fighting proficiency. Good targets for these counter-strikes are the hands and face, as minimal power is required to effectively injure or stun the enemy.

In this avoidance-and-counterattack method, timing is crucial to success. The countering move must be made precisely as the adversary begins his attack. The ninja's powers of observation and judgment must be very sharp to anticipate his attacker's movement. Any hesitation will result in lost time, and put the ninja in a position requiring defensive blocking.

CANES WITH CONCEALED WEAPONS

The hour of our ninjutsu demonstration for the Tokyo Metropolitan Police Department had arrived. Our show had been preceded by demonstrations of judo, traditional Japanese swordsmanship, kendo, and two types of karate, and it had been interesting to watch the other disciplines in action. The demonstrations had been arranged to complement one another, and

sporting methods, with constant interruptions for the award-
ing of points and the proclaiming of winners, alternated with historical methods, ritualistic and precise in their slow deliberateness.
The master had warned me that our presentation would be quite
different from the others. I now understood what he had meant.

We all burst onto the polished wooden floor and warmed up
with handsprings and rolls while Hatsumi Sensei took a position
by the microphone. He gave a brief explanation of historical ninjutsu and its philosophy, stressing the difference between what he
called "comic-book and TV ninja" and the true practitioners of
the ancient mystic art. The audience of police officers and reporters was quietly attentive.

We bowed and the demonstration began. Scene after scene unfolded, as teams of ninja clashed with their oppressors. It was indeed a show, and reflected Hatsumi Sensei's years of experience
as a technical adviser to selected Japanese historical films.

My scene involved a clash between the forces of government
and religion in ancient Japan. I was playing the part of a ninja
disguised as a wandering Buddhist monk, and a fellow student
was taking the role of a village samurai upholding Shinto, the
state religion. I had been given a black robe, a string of prayer
beads, a shoulder-high cane, and a rubber scalp piece as my costume. My nemesis wore a short coat, samurai leggings, and two
swords tucked in his sash. Hatsumi Sensei set the scene, describing
to the audience how we happened to meet on a road outside an
imaginary village.

My attacker drew his long sword with a yell, and advanced
menacingly toward me. Being a mere monk with a wooden cane,
I slid back into a defensive position, clutching the string of wooden
beads in my right hand. I shifted about, looking for an escape,
until I was against the wall with nowhere to go. He slowly raised
the sword above his head, preparing for a downward cut.

As he stepped forward into the slash, I flung the beaded cord
at his ankles. The beads spread to form a large circle in the air,

humming as they whirled out to tangle the attacker's legs. The samurai leaped into the air, pulling his knees high to clear his feet from the bead lasso. While his attention was diverted, I slipped by him and out into open space again.

Our script called for three lunging slashes and a final clash. On the first slash, I sidestepped and slammed the end of my cane into the back of his hand gripping the sword. The samurai pivoted and brought the sword across my midsection, while I blocked his cut by positioning the cane vertically in front of my body. Bits of wood flew into the air as I braced against the blade when it hit. I backed away from him, rolling the cane in my right hand, forming a large figure-eight pattern in front of me. The samurai attacked with a third slash, which I caught with a diagonally braced cane, my hands gripping each end of the wooden weapon.

We separated and positioned ourselves for the final clash. The samurai yelled and charged with a diagonal slash to the left side of my neck. I lifted my cane into position along my left side and deflected the blade to a safe area. I then snapped my right wrist in a pulling motion on the cane and the wood separated a quarter of the way from the end, as I pulled a long straight sword blade from the center of the hollow cane. With a circular motion to my right, I brought the blade down in a dragging cut along my attacker's left collarbone and shoulder. I put my body weight behind the attack, and he tumbled backward with its force.

The samurai howled in mock pain and then slumped to the floor as I jumped backward clutching my blade. As he formed a pile on the polished wood, I reassembled my cane-sword, picked up my beads, and moved off the demonstration floor as called for by the script.

The *shinobi-zue* (ninja cane) had the appearance of an ordinary walking stick, farmer's staff, or priest's baton. Inside the cane, however, was concealed a wide array of fighting tools.

Some canes contained hidden knives, varying in length from

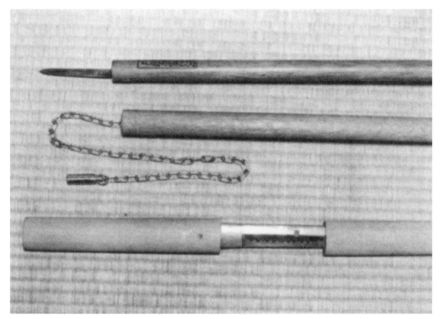

41. Canes containing hidden weapons.

daggers to full sword blades. Part of the cane actually formed the hilt of the sword in some cases, while in others the blade could be removed for throwing. Special end caps could be removed from some long canes, exposing a fixed blade and turning the device into a spear.

Other ninja canes were hollowed out to conceal chains running their full length. The links easily collapsed and folded into each other inside the hollow cane and, when released, would reach a yard or more beyond the range of the ordinary staff. The chain was normally attached to an iron weight or hook which was used as a secret weapon in combat. The chain could be released suddenly to snake out and strike an adversary or entangle his limbs and weapons.

Once converted to a blade or chain weapon, the cane was utilized with the same fighting skills used in ninja blade or chain

42(a)–(c). The cane becomes a fighting blade.

fighting. A ninja who was especially adept at fighting with chains would carry one inside a *shinobi-zue,* whereas a skilled swordsman or knife thrower would carry a concealed blade.

Another specialized group of canes was hollowed out to be used for shooting darts or blinding powders at the enemy. By removing both end caps, the ninja could use his weapon as a blowgun or smokescreen generator. Other tube canes had one removable cap only, and were gripped in one hand and waved with a flinging motion to propel the contents at the attacker.

87

THE NINJA SWORD

The summer sun rose over the flat farm country northeast of Tokyo. Dawn had come at an incredibly early hour, and my teacher and I had risen with the sun to begin our training. We walked along the narrow raised pathways that separated the flooded rice fields. The teacher was carrying a long canvas bag that contained some sort of training gear. I could not tell exactly what was in the bag and, though curious, I decided to wait for the teacher to disclose the contents when he was ready.

The brilliant sun shone through the pure air and summer humidity with a steely white quality, bleaching out the colors of the new day. The cloudless sky, the calm surface of the water surrounding us, the weathered stone grave-markers ahead of us, everything seemed to be reflecting, or consumed by, the dazzling whiteness of the sun. There was a numbing, hypnotizing effect to the scene, and my body fought it with a feeling of inner agitation and restlessness.

Three crows came winging out of the woods at the edge of the fields. Even their glistening black plumage turned to the ubiquitous silver-white colorless color of the sun. They were huge birds, and their cawing momentarily diverted my attention from the teacher and my purpose for being there.

When I turned to face the teacher, I was stunned by a beam of blazing light as intense as the morning sun behind me. The searing rays were blinding, and seemed to emanate from a source in front of the teacher's chest. I could see him dimly, moving behind a fiery white ball that flickered and bounced up and down.

I was captivated. I began to move toward the teacher, to inspect the source of the white blaze more clearly. The light suddenly vanished, and the teacher shouted for me to freeze where I was. We both held our positions for a few seconds, as my eyes slowly recovered from the dazzling onslaught. I could see that I had stopped about 8 inches from the tip of a sword blade pointed at

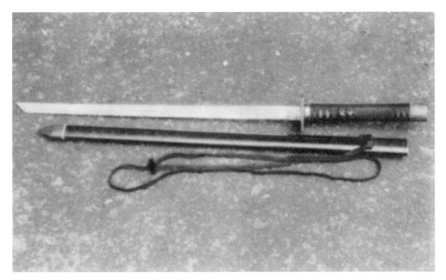

43. Ninja sword and scabbard.

my face. As my gaze slid along the length of the sword, I realized that the ball of light had merely been the sun, reflected on the polished steel of the weapon. The light had gone out when the teacher leveled the weapon on my approach. With a bit of awe, I wondered just how many lights had been permanently extinguished by that blade in generations past.

Bladed weapons were the ninja's primary fighting tools. Many variations of the blade were utilized in combat. The ninja used his sword for close-range fighting, his spear or halberd for fighting at a moderate distance, and throwing blades for distant targets.

The ninja sword was normally shorter in length than the samurai sword of the period. The *ninja-to* was more like a utilitarian bush knife, and served many purposes in addition to fighting. Where the samurai families cherished their swords and sought out the finest swordsmiths, the ninja considered his blade a mere tool and did not attribute any spirit or soul to it. The important

44. Standard two-hand sword grip.

tsuba (hand guard) of the ninja's sword was generally forged from a large piece of steel. It was rarely adorned or engraved as were the samurai hand-guards.

The sword hilt and scabbard were normally nonreflective black in color, and were worn in the sash edge-up, along the left side of the body. Occasionally the sword and scabbard were worn in the back of the sash or strapped over the shoulder to hide the sword or make climbing easier.

For standard use, the sword is gripped with the right hand just below the *tsuba* and the left hand just above the end. A gap is left between the hands to permit flexibility when moving the sword about. Specialized sword grips include the single right-hand grip, useful for fighting with the sword while climbing, running, moving through difficult terrain, or carrying things in the left hand. In

45. Using the reverse single-hand grip.

the reverse single-hand grip, a rather unorthodox method favored by ninja, the hilt is held so that the blade extends backward along the arm for concealment, instead of pointing forward.

The first goal of ninja swordsmanship training is to develop the ability to draw the sword in defense with sufficient speed to cut the attacker without having to first block his initial slash. The drawing action actually turns into the first cut, as opposed to the technique of drawing and then preparing to cut. This skill is practiced as a response to a surprise attack, and the cut is directed to the attacker's leading arm, body, or neck. If the attacker's slash should be too advanced, the draw is turned into a block.

46. Sword against shuko.

Slashing cuts generally utilize the tip or last quarter of the blade. The cutting movements are fast and light, as though the tip of the blade were pulling the sword and hands. Heavy power movements, as those used in swinging a baseball bat, are not a part of the ninja's sword method. The sword should feel as though it were an extension of the arms, moving with natural power and grace.

Along with the fast-draw cuts, students of ninjutsu also practice fencing skills in which the drawn sword is used against an attacker's sword or another weapon. Just as in the unarmed fighting method, the body follows the guideline of naturalness of movement, merging with and overcoming the attacker's actions.

There is no windup or draw back and pause before executing a strike, and there should be no perceptible break between preparation and the actual cutting motion. Raising the blade up dramatically before the cut would warn the adversary, as would drawing a fist back threateningly before punching.

Thrusting strikes have a stabbing or plunging motion when directed at body or head targets. The thrust can also be used with a sawing or slicing action to attack the limbs or outside edges of the body. A slice to the wrist, arm, shoulder, or lower leg can prevent the adversary from continuing the fight.

THROWING BLADES

It was early evening in a wooded stretch of rural Japan. The sun was well on its way down, and all the foliage reflected its golden orange light, which made the shadows so intense and alive. I crouched in the low wild shrubs, my back resting against the rough bark of a tree trunk. A light breeze played through the branches and fluttered the fabric of my black training outfit. Animal noises and bird calls occasionally rang out through the stillness, as I kept my breathing light and listened for the signal.

At last I heard the ragged, throaty cries of a crow over to my right. It sounded just like any other crow except that it called four times, the number pronounced *shi* in Japanese which also means "death." It was in reality my teacher, and it was the signal I had been awaiting.

Along with my eight fellow team members, I poked my head above the foliage and scanned the area. There was the target over to the left, a tree with a white strip of cloth tied around it. Together with my right arm, eight other arms simultaneously rose in the air. Together with my arm, eight other arms simultaneously snapped straight down and pointed at the target. Nine

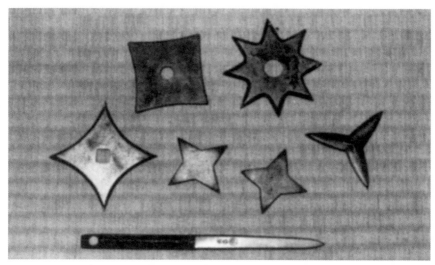

47. Several types of shuriken.

thin blades slid from nine hands and slammed into the tree before us with a humming ring. We heard the crow caw one more
time, and then we all moved back into hiding while the white
band was moved to a new target.

The ninja's throwing knife is called a *shuriken*. This weapon can
take countless shapes, but there are two basic types: straight-
bladed and multipointed. The straight *shuriken* vary in size from
short needles to broad knives. Some take the shape of long narrow
spikes, while others are flat and wide in construction. The multipointed star or square *shuriken* are cut from a single piece of steel,
and have anywhere from three to eight points radiating from the
center. The *shuriken* are usually carried in groups of nine, concealed in hidden pockets inside the ninja's jacket or leggings.

Historically, the Togakure-ryu used a four-pointed throwing
blade called a *semban shuriken*, in addition to the straight knife.
The square blade can be used accurately up to 30 feet from the
target, and can also be held in the hand for close-range fighting.

94

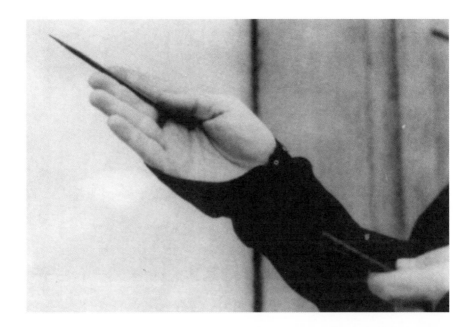

48(a), (b). Gripping the shuriken for throwing.

49(a), (b). Gripping and throwing the semban shuriken.

The square or star *shuriken* were used primarily for wounding or harrassing the enemy. The shallowness of the points usually prevented them from penetrating deeply enough to kill. However, the weapon was very effective when thrown into the hands or face of an armed pursuer by surprise.

The star *shuriken* could also take the role of an "invisible attacker." If a guard or enemy stood out in a cleared area, the ninja hidden in shrubs or beside a wall would throw the star blade in a spinning manner. The blades would cut the startled adversary and fly off into the grass or dirt out of sight. The bewildered victim, having been slashed by an invisible swordsman, would then take off to seek help, leaving the area unguarded.

In combat, the square or star blade is gripped at its outermost edge by the points and thrown on a level horizontal plane. The *shuriken* is held lightly on the fingers, with the wrist held straight and the arm bent at the elbow but relaxed. The arm is straightened in the direction of the target, and the blade allowed to slip from the grasp. The blade derives its power from the snap of the hand and forearm as a unit, and the wrist should not be flipped or bent during the throw. A similar straight-wristed fling is used for the straight-bladed *shuriken*.

5 ✦ *THE WAY OF INVISIBILITY*

The car's headlights probed through total blackness as we carefully proceeded along a narrow gravel trail. My teacher was driving, and another student and I were the passengers. We had followed the crest of the retaining levee along the Edo River and were now making our way down the slope to what I remembered as being a golf course.

The car came to a halt quietly. Peering out the window, I could see nothing but the tiny headlights of cars passing along the Noda Bridge in the distance. There was no moon at all, and there seemed to be no stars. The teacher turned off the ignition and commented that we would meet some of the other students behind the ninth tee.

I had been right: it was a golf course. "In America we don't have the opportunity to train this way. It's illegal to be on a golf course like this at night. The security patrols would run you off or have the police arrest you."

"Well, of course. It is the same in Japan. You have to stay aware and alert this way. It is part of the training."

I was more than a little surprised. "What would happen if they did catch you?"

"We never worry about that. They never catch us. They couldn't. They never even know we are out here."

We had parked behind some high wild grass and shrubs to conceal the car. The teacher and the other student disappeared ahead of me into the blackness, moving through the grass toward the open tee area. I hurried after them, knowing that if I got lost here, I'd never find my way home until sunrise. The wild plant growth was incredibly thick. Branches and exposed roots grabbed at me with every move I attempted. I had been working at moving through the tangle for a few minutes, when I heard the sound of a light splash. A half second later I felt the cool, heavy flow of water saturating my left boot.

As I pulled my foot from the water, a quiet voice from my right startled me. "You must be more careful. You are making far too much noise."

"I'm sorry. I couldn't see the water here."

"No, it's too dark to see. You must smell the water," the teacher replied. "Do not breathe through your mouth as you are doing. Use your nose. Take a deep breath and exhale it all, then use quick, shallow breathing until you need another deep breath. As each whiff of air passes through your nose, concentrate on the inside of your nostrils, at the top, right below the eyes. That is where you will notice any changes in smell."

"Well, the next time we come here, I'll be on the lookout for the water," I laughed quietly, as I tried to squeeze some of the wetness from the canvas of my *tabi*.

"We will not be coming here again. Hatsumi Sensei does not want us to use the same training area twice."

"You have never been here before?"

"No. If we trained in the same place too often, we would become used to the surroundings and lose the necessity for awareness. You must learn to move without being detected through all kinds of terrain: water, grass, loose gravel, hillsides, carpeting. This could be crucial for victory in combat."

SENSE DECEPTION

In beginning a study of the ninja's invisibility methods, one should first explore methods of deceiving the senses of the enemy. The sense of sight is perhaps the most crucial to anyone engaged in searching, scouting, or guarding. Therefore, the ninja must employ a wide range of techniques to confound the enemy's vision. Methods of camouflage involve disguise, concealment, or alteration of appearance to render the ninja difficult to see or identify. Methods of confusion such as visual distraction, the contrast between bright light and darkness, and optical illusion can be used to divert the observer's attention.

The sense of smell is perhaps the weakest in most humans, so men compensate by using dogs to detect their enemy's presence through odor. Therefore, the ninja must be careful about wind patterns, staying downwind or disguising his smell.

Sounds can be used to deceive the sense of hearing. There are certain crackling or rustling sounds that cannot be avoided in a wild area, so advantage must be taken of other noises to cover one's movements. Traffic, machinery, or conversation can mask footfalls. As we stood in deep brush at the edge of the golf course, the teacher told us that we would use the sound of the wind to conceal ourselves.

We waited a few seconds, and sure enough, a low wind that I hadn't noticed before moved from left to right, swaying and rattling the grass and reeds. "We must move swiftly now," the teacher commented. "Be careful how you move your feet."

PHANTOM STEPS

Japan's historical ninja were famous for their ability to move undetected through the use of a series of special walking techniques. Each technique requires long and diligent practice until complete mastery of the body's movement is attained.

50. Master of sense deception, a ninja watches from concealing foliage.

51. Ko ashi.

Ko Ashi (Small Step)

This small, stabbing step is used to move silently through shallow water or dry leaves. The object of the technique is to get the foot beneath the surface of the water or leaves without causing noise. The ninja maintains a low hip position with the body weight on the front foot, pulls the rear foot up, and lets it glide over the spot where it will touch down. The toe is then pointed downward and dug straight in, passing through the surface slowly. After the heel has gone through the surface, the foot is leveled out so that the sole of the foot may come to rest on the ground beneath the water or leaves. Weight shifts onto this new leading foot, as the trailing foot is pulled out and moved forward into the next step. This walking technique gives the ninja the appearance of a crane picking its way through wild terrain.

52(a), (b). Yoko aruki.

Yoko Aruki (Sideways Walking)

This technique is for moving stealthily in the shadows of buildings and negotiating tight passageways. The hips are lined up with, rather than facing in, the direction of travel, and the stepping motion is lateral. The movement begins by leading with the hips to one side or the other, depending on whether one is advancing or retreating. As the weight shifts to the leading leg, the knees are bent deeply and the rear leg crosses over in front. The body weight then shifts to the new leading foot, as the new rear leg is pulled from behind and repositioned in the lead. The sideways walking motion is done in a smooth and level flowing action, and gives the ninja the appearance of a sand crab scurrying sideways across a beach.

103

Nuki Ashi (Sweeping Step)

This technique permits the ninja to cross wooden planks or straw matting undetected by giving him complete control of his body weight. From a low crouching position, the balance and then the body weight are slowly shifted to the forward leg until it supports the entire body. The rear leg is then pulled forward and in toward the supporting leg. The ankles barely brush each other as the moving leg goes forward and out with the toes pointing slightly inward. With the weight on the stationary leg, the outside edge of the moving foot can be used as a feeler to probe lightly for any obstacles that might be in the way. The foot is then eased to the floor, outer edge first. The weight is gently shifted to this foot, and can be withdrawn quickly if any creaking of the floor is noticed. This groping foot then becomes the new support foot as the ninja continues forward. With his hands moving lightly like tentacles, the ninja takes on the appearance of an octopus feeling his way across the ocean floor.

53(a)–(c). Nuki ashi.

To test our effectiveness in the walking techniques, newspapers were spread over the wooden floor of the dojo. The papers were several sheets thick, and long and wide enough so that it took several steps to move from one end to the other. The paper was then thoroughly drenched, so that missteps or slips would show up as tears or folds in the wet paper. While crossing the fragile wet suface, we were shown how to practice relaxed breathing rather than holding our breath. In addition to encouraging naturalness of movement, normal breathing helps to prevent gasping when balance or proper footing is temporarily lost.

Beyond the dozen or so walking techniques, the ninja also practices stealth in all other activities to develop a total demeanor of precision and awareness. The training begins with short practice periods. At random points during the day, the student attempts to perform all normal actions as silently as possible for approximately 5 minutes. Small hand-held objects are put down by touching the hand to the surface first, and then lowering the object into place. When sitting or standing, notice is taken of body weight and balance to avoid flopping or jerking motions. When moving a larger object, it is important to use only as much strength as is necessary, to avoid moving the object too far. The student learns what causes undue noise so that he can avoid that type of movement if possible. He develops a consciousness of all noises he makes, and a better perspective on his relationship with his environment.

RECONNAISSANCE

The teacher and I were joined at the edge of the rough growth by the third member of our team. In front of us towered the stone retaining wall at the edge of the golf course, and we crouched in the blackness at the foot of the wall between some trees that grew alongside. The darkness made it difficult to determine exactly where we were in relation to our rendezvous point.

54. Climbing a tree with the shuko.

The teacher said that he would check our bearings and slipped a pair of *shuko* on his hands as he stood up. The broad iron bands wrapped around the palms and backs of his hands, with four sharp spikes protruding from the palm beneath the fingers. A wrist-support ring was tethered to the spiked band by a wide strap of leather, which served to protect the skin of the hands. With a small leap the teacher sprang onto a tree, gripping with a clawed hand and the sole of a foot on either side of the trunk. He then continued up the tree with the light, agile movements of a squirrel, digging the spikes in and pulling them free to move his body upward. He was into the branches in a matter of seconds, and from there he scanned the landscape.

The teacher then braced himself by entwining his legs in the branches, and produced a small bundle from inside his jacket. He made a throwing motion in the direction of the wall, and I could see a cord fly out through his hands. He tugged on the cord of the *kaginawa* to make sure that the hook at its end held securely, pulling the treetop in the direction of the wall. He then released the cord, which dropped along the rocks of the wall, and lowered himself down the trunk of the tree.

We took turns scrambling up the wall using the rope for guidance and our feet to propel us upward over the rock surface. At the top, the three of us moved easily onto the level surface of the ninth tee.

BLENDING WITH THE NIGHT

As we approached the center of the grassy expanse, a low voice called out in quiet greeting. The effect was jolting. Four dim figures rose from the ground like wraiths from the grave. They were clothed in traditional black ninja garb and had blended into the darkness perfectly. They had appeared only when they had wished us to become aware of them.

The *shinobi shozoku* (the ninja's traditional outfit) is made up of split-toed *tabi*, special trousers that tie onto the body, a jacket with overlapping lapels tucked into the trousers, protective arm-and-hand sleeves, and a tied scarf that serves as a combination mask and hood. The outfit is made of tough, dark-colored cotton fabric, fitted loosely. This gives the ninja freedom of movement, and an ability to blend in with the night shadows.

We began our training that evening with unarmed fighting practice, moving in and out of a rough circle and working our

55. Traditional ninja outfit.

way from one opponent to the next. Unseen feet and hands battered me in the darkness. I swung but could not connect. No matter how hard I tried, I could not land a punch on my opponents.

Something was pulling at my jacket, and suddenly my foot was swept from beneath me. I hit the soft ground and rolled to cushion the fall. It was so dark that I could barely tell which way was up when I stood to reposition myself for combat. "I feel as though I were the punching bag tonight," I commented wearily as I assumed a fighting pose in front of my next training partner.

There was a chuckle from the darkness. "You will continue to be the punching bag as long as you keep that high body pose. You are moving around like a boxer in a ring. There is no way

109

that you can see your attackers that way; they just blend in with the ground. Lower your hips.''

I dropped my pose, and was amazed to see my opponents silhouetted against the night sky. With this simple adjustment of my fighting attitude, I was able to discern dark forms blotting out stars that I hadn't noticed before. The training continued, and I was able to handle the situation more effectively with my newfound vision. I could see the figures darting toward me and to my sides. Punches were thrown and intercepted. Kicks were knocked away with counterkicks.

ATTACKING THE EYES

I was holding a relaxed fighting position across from a black-garbed opponent. My lower body position allowed me to see him, and judge that he was 8 or 9 feet away from me. My opponent held a relaxed position also, and we studied each other silently. The darkness and black training suits made it impossible to tell with whom I was fighting. I had no idea whether I was facing a student who was my junior, or the head instructor himself. Hatsumi Sensei had told me that in such situations one must "feel" the intention of the adversary in order to know what to do. Unfortunately, my lack of sensitivity at that time only allowed me to feel an overwhelming sense of indecision as to proper strategy. For the time being, anyway, my opponent was too far away from me to be of any danger.

Suddenly, from 9 feet away, I felt the stranger touch my eyelids. He didn't move his body at all, but merely reached out with his hand. The pressure was not painful; in fact, the touch was quite light and gentle. But it was such a surprise that I jerked my head back and to the right in automatic reaction. As I pulled my head back, my body straightened up and I lost my low posture. I felt a foot hit my leg out from under me as fists knocked my arms aside. Unseen punches and kicks assailed my body,

56. Smoke bomb used to blind the enemy.

and all I could do was leap backward and roll away to avoid the onslaught.

At first, the teacher laughingly refused to explain how my opponent had done what was seemingly impossible. I was admonished to simply not let my guard down the next time. With further coaxing, however, he finally admitted that it had been a trick. My opponent had merely tossed a small handful of grass at my eyes. Though it had not hurt at all, it had certainly been a surprise and diverted my attention from the fight.

The ninja's *metsubushi* (blinding powders) could confound an enemy's vision. They were commonly carried in small packets inside the ninja's jacket, and usually consisted of a mixture of ashes, ground pepper, and sand. If a ninja were outnumbered or surrounded, he could fling the *metsubushi* mixture into the faces of his attackers and leave them swimming in a thick gray cloud. Heat-sensitive smoke bombs could accomplish the same effect, and the ninja often tossed them into campfires or heating stoves when making an escape.

111

THE ART OF DISGUISE

The historical ninja were masters of another means of hiding themselves from the gaze of others, the *shichiho-de* (seven disguises). When it was necessary to infiltrate an area or a camp, the ninja would use the obvious technique of blending in with the surrounding community so as not to be detected by the enemy. Beyond merely disguising himself with a costume, the ninja would totally impersonate the character he adopted, in speech, mannerisms, and knowledge.

Historically, the seven most commonly used disguises were the following:

> *Yamabushi* (mountain warrior-priest)
> *Sarugaku* (actor or entertainer)
> *Komuso* (traveling priest)
> *Ronin* (wandering samurai for hire)
> *Akindo* (merchant)
> *Hokashi* (musician)
> *Shukke* (Buddhist monk)

But the ninja was by no means limited to these seven identities. If more appropriate, the ninja might appear as a doctor, tramp, farmer, soldier, fisherman, or anything else.

The ninja was taught to pick an identity in which he appeared to fit readily. Dramatic uses of makeup and disguise are fun to watch on television, but could have been deadly mistakes in reality. Age, for example, was very important. A young person might have found it hard to pose as a merchant, whereas an older person would have found it difficult to play the role of an apprentice. Skin texture, especially of the hands, was crucial also. It is unlikely that a rich man would have had battered, suntanned hands; and a fair-skinned individual with well-manicured hands could have drawn skepticism posing as the gardener on an estate. Careful observation of dressing habits and clothing fashions helped the ninja fit his role.

Any character role had a natural area of expertise accompanying it, either in terms of intellectual knowledge or physical skills. The successful ninja selected a suitable role for his own personality and background. Obviously, some identities required more knowledge than others, and therefore took longer to prepare for. The well-trained ninja used as few words as possible, realizing that the more he said, the greater the chance of the listener detecting a mistake in details.

Some character roles had a familiarity with places and customs as part of their makeup. The wise ninja selected a background with which he had a natural tie, as details could be deadly to the unsure. If questioned, a fisherman had to know the coastline, a merchant the location of his shop and those of his suppliers and rivals. The ninja also had to know his way around the area of operation. For this he needed a working knowledge of local streets, corridors, gates, forest tracts, bodies of water, and means of transportation.

The voice quality and type of language used had to be appropriate for the character being assumed. Accents, dialects, slang, and technical jargon were observed and studied to guard against misuse.

In using one of the *shichiho-de,* the most important psychological factor to keep in mind was to maintain alertness in an outwardly calm fashion that would not draw attention. When a ninja assumed an identity he actually became the new character, and others could not tell that it was a disguise unless he told them, or he gave himself away by misusing details. When people are studied in their everyday activities, an unconscious thoughtless manner will be noticed in most of their actions. An auto mechanic does not think about acting like an auto mechanic, nor does the loan officer at the bank strive to capture the essence of acting like a loan officer. They are people going about their routines and chores of the day. If suddenly confronted and accused of not really being auto mechanics or loan officers, they would regard the accuser as a mere pest or fool and continue with their work. The ninja attained the same artless naturalness when assuming an identity. As in physical combat, the ninja did not fear the enemy. He was simply aware of him and his powers, and took appropriate precautions.

6 ✦ *SHADOW WARRIORS*

The training hall in the master's home, in which I studied ninjutsu with the other students, was small by Western standards. The tiny room was paneled in wood and had a polished wooden floor. All throws, leaps, and rolls were done on the bare floor to prepare the students for the reality outside the dojo. Racks and pegs along the walls held all sorts of weapons: some made for training and some the actual tools of combat. Spears, chains, swords, sticks, ropes, and grappling hooks all covered the walls in a disarray of weathered wood and antique steel. Miniature shrines looked down on the training area from shelves built close to the high-beamed ceiling.

In one corner hung a large picture of Hatsumi Sensei training with his teacher, Toshitsugu Takamatsu. Takamatsu Sensei, the thirty-third master of the Togakure-ryu, had lived in Nara, in the region of Iga, where ninjutsu first came into being. He had died a few years before I came to Japan, and I knew him only through the stories and photographs in our training hall.

Takamatsu Sensei was part of a generation of Japanese that had grown up knowing only war. When Japan opened her doors to the Western world in the 1800s, it seemed that imperialism was the way the Western nations had grown strong. The Japanese moved to join the rest of the world in territorial expansion to protect the homeland, and became involved in a series of wars as the result.

Though Takamatsu Sensei was never in the Japanese military, war was his world and its waging was his skill. One of my teachers told me that Takamatsu Sensei would never have accepted me for training, for he felt that foreigners could not understand an art so closely tied to the culture of Japan and the wars that had shaped it.

For someone like Takamatsu Sensei, especially during his travels alone throughout Southeast Asia, it was of the utmost importance to protect the secrets of the ninja. So thoroughly did he conceal his background in ninjutsu that his own neighbors knew nothing of it until they read of it in his obituaries. In this respect he perhaps reincarnated the ninja of old, for whom secrecy was a matter of life and death.

War has always been the arena in which ninja could make their greatest contributions, and always through clandestine methods. Historically, the ninja's most important roles were in the shadows, as espionage agents and commandos.

ESPIONAGE

The ninja approach to warfare was in dramatic contrast with other arts of war of the period. Whereas Chinese texts conceived of strength primarily in terms of numbers, the ninja held that victory is more essentially determined by the relative quality and determination of the combatants, and the timing of the conflict. The most successful commander was thought to be the one who could work with the unfolding of history in such a way as to attain his goals without the costly depletion of resources or the needless sacrifice of lives. Guided by this philosophy, the ninja mystics of the Iga and Koga wilderness developed the arts of deception and espionage as the most effective means of insuring peace and security, as opposed to the samurai outlook that relished the glory of a dramatic battle leading to total victory.

Throughout the centuries of Japanese history, it was the responsibility of Togakure-ryu *jonin* like Tatsumori Togakure, Takakumo Togakure, and Gobei Toda to be thoroughly familiar with methods of directing espionage activities on a broad scale. When committing themselves to any intelligence-gathering activity, the ninja would observe six major considerations for successful espionage. These six principles, taken in order, also formed a plan of action.

1. Planting Agents

As the first consideration, the ninja agent and his organization had to be unknown and undetected. To this end the ninja worked at maintaining a low profile, reminding himself that a favorable outcome to his endeavor depended upon his ability to draw no attention to himself or his purpose. The effective espionage agent appeared to be one of the common people, an everyday sort who would be unsuspected by all. Therefore, the first step was to set up an organization that was powerful and yet unknown.

As guidelines there evolved a group of fundamental approaches to planting *genin* agents in areas of effectiveness. The five basic manifestations of all things, which can be utilized in individual combat (see pp. 55, 136), also had application to this aspect of espionage. The five approaches to spy placement, based on the five manifestations, offered a range of possibilities to fit a variety of circumstances.

Chi (Earth) Approach. This involved the careful prior placement of reliable spies on whom effective action could later depend. This earth approach to the systematic building of stability is reflected in such English-language idioms as "gaining a firm foothold" or "getting in on the ground floor."

An efficient *jonin* would plant agents in all territories with which he might deal. The agent was sent to his target area during peaceful and relaxed times, when it was easy for him to become a member of the community and pick up a normal life routine. Once in location, the ninja would then go about cultivating appropriate contacts and getting to know his way around the area. Prior to becoming involved in direct action, the ninja might spend his time gathering up bits of information from conversations, observation, or reading just so that he could have as much knowledge as possible at his disposal.

A ninja could also be sent into the enemy's territory as prewar tensions built or conflict erupted. With the urgency of the coming clash and the feeling of crisis in the community, the ninja would slip into place unnoticed. The agent could seek a position with some key wartime trade, in communications, or in the military forces themselves. Background checks would be more difficult during periods of crisis as time and manpower were at a premium.

Sui (Water) Approach. The basis of this approach was to encourage in the enemy feelings of increased power and personal satisfaction with life, by appealing to his emotions. This flexible strategy of adaptation to the adversary aimed at creating the impression of security in his mind, while actually undermining him.

The ninja might allow one of their agents to be captured, knowing that the agent would be interrogated for information. The sacrificed agent would be supplied with false information that at length he would divulge. The enemy would then be guided by the fabrications obtained from the spy. Many times the captured agent did not realize that he was carrying false information, and he would fight convincingly to keep his secret knowledge from the enemy.

Women could be used to play up to weaknesses in the enemy's key personnel, through either indirect psychological or direct physical means. The *kunoichi* was trained in a manner similar

57. Kunoichi displays a mystic hand position.

to her male counterparts, although the training of women emphasized the less tangible aspects of personal warfare. Skills of psychology, intuition, and the manipulation of another's personality
took precedence over battlefield tactics in the women's education.
Though female ninja were at least given basic instruction in
ninjutsu fighting methods, their most reliable combat techniques
were surprise attacks to weak points of the body, and often utilized
concealed blades, the elaborate hairpins that were then in fashion,

119

or ingenious sexual toys and musical instruments that could be transformed into killing weapons.

Shimma kunoichi were actual members of the ninja family, brought up and trained for their specific careers in espionage. These women were directed by a male *kantokusha* (commander), who usually tried to give each female agent the impression that she was his only *kunoichi*. Careful guidance of these female spies, with their emotional and intuitive natures heightened through sensitivity training, was needed to prevent them from actually falling in love with their targets, or losing sight of the ultimate purpose for which they were fighting.

Karima kunoichi were not members of the family, but were hired on a temporary basis for specific jobs. Women such as maids, mistresses, or entertainers who had ready access to an enemy commander might be tempted to do the ninja's bidding for the right price or other motivation. Other women such as artists, fortune-tellers, or prostitutes, who could create the opportunity to get near the enemy, could also be hired by the ninja if it were appropriate for his overall strategy.

Ka (Fire) Approach. This could be seen in spy-placement ruses that directly moved against the enemy forces by aggressively using the enemy's own people for their downfall. This fighting-fire-with-fire approach relied on the exploitation of weaknesses within the enemy's own organization through direct confrontation.

In more difficult areas to place an agent, the ninja might recruit a local citizen who was already a member of the enemy's community. The local might be disenchanted with his government or a sympathizer with the ninja's cause. Those aspiring to great wealth or influence might also be candidates for the position of local agent. These locals, being known and recognized, could move about their community easily without causing suspicion. The use of local citizens as agents was especially popular when the ninja organization had to operate in an area where language or physical characteristics made infiltration impossible.

Though difficult to recruit, the enemy's own key personnel could become very effective agents. Naturally, the higher the defector's rank in the enemy hierarchy, the more valuable he could be to the ninja's cause. The enemy's people might be persuaded to become agents through promises of wealth, power, or other gain, or through blackmail, threats, or fear. Once he had made the commitment to betrayal, the spy stayed in the service of his former leader while giving information and assistance to the ninja.

Fu (Wind) Approach. This was characterized by harmonious interaction with others, and a quality of being everywhere at the same time. This strategy used the enemy's own moves and devices to defeat him, and allowed the ninja clan to achieve victory with a minimum of direct combat activity.

After an enemy agent had been detected in the area of operation, he might be supplied with false or inaccurate information that he would relay to his superiors. Occasionally he would be supplied with harmless true data so that his supervisors would think that he was still undetected. When this enemy agent outgrew his usefulness, he would be captured or fed false information that would discredit him in the eyes of his own superiors.

A ninja agent could appear to desert his own side and go over to the enemy. He would then convince the enemy of his sincerity and go to work for them. Posing as a traitor to his own side, the ninja would actually be supplying his *chunin* or *jonin* with crucial data. He might even pose as a spy for the enemy, and send back some verifiable facts mixed with misleading information. In a variation on the double-agent role, some independent ninja actually did work for both sides. Posing as a loyal spy, the agent sold secrets to both sides at the same time, in order to manipulate the playing out of events and control the balance of power.

Ku (Void) Approach. The formless emptiness that provides the potentiality of everything was the guiding principle here. The creative use of potential and making the best of surprise developments characterized these spy-placement methods.

A spy who had infiltrated the forces of the enemy often worked faithfully for some time to establish his trustworthiness, without engaging actively in espionage that could expose him. He bided his time until he received a predetermined signal, which actualized his potential by sending him into action from within the enemy's ranks.

A captured ninja might cooperate with his captors so as to remain of use to his side in the future. He might claim no loyalty other than money and appear to sell out to the enemy. Cut off completely from his organization, the ninja in this situation aimed first at just staying alive until he could escape or return to active duty.

2. Determining Goals

Once the agent had been established in his area of operation, the next step was to find out the aims of the enemy. To simply spy on a group without knowing its goals is pointless and of no value. When armed with the knowledge of what the enemy intended to do, the ninja could effectively go about his job of obtaining detailed, useful information.

3. Determining Strategy

After establishing what the goals of the enemy were, the ninja would next set out to determine his strategy and resources. Key people, target dates, communication codes, means of support, and the enemy's espionage system were all of interest to the agent.

4. Sowing Confusion

The ninja's next step was to cause confusion in the enemy's ranks. When possible he would feed false or misleading information to the enemy. This could be done directly, perhaps by posing as a double agent, or indirectly, by allowing agents of the opposition to discover the false information. Another effective tactic was the creation of dissension among key personnel by means of rumor, falsified communications, or playing one man's personal aims off against those of another.

5. Determining Tactics

The ninja would next work to learn the enemy's fighting tactics and strong points. Troop placement and movement, numbers, logistics and support, and favorite or secret combat techniques were all ferreted out by the agent. The *genin* could study past conflicts or observe actual drills to uncover these important bits of military information.

6. Counterespionage

The final duty of the espionage agent was to keep his own side's tactics concealed and unpredictable. The ninja was in a good position to learn just how much the enemy knew about his own army's strengths and tactics. It was his duty to alert his home forces when the enemy was on to their plans, codes, or favorite combat techniques.

Concealment

While the espionage agent was living within the territory of the enemy, every day presented countless possibilities for accidents or small mistakes that could result in discovery and execution. Therefore, the ninja created a wide buffer of protective devices to help conceal his true identity and allow him to function effectively.

Many ninja maintained multiple identities, and some actually had more than one family and home. By living several lives at the same time, the ninja could create the impression of being everywhere at once, and could have all the resources and contacts

58. Concealed storage compartment in a ninja house.

of several different individuals. By psychologically jumping back and forth from one reality to another, the ninja kept himself mentally alert and provided himself with varying perspectives from which to evaluate all actions and events.

Specially constructed ninja houses incorporated security devices of sometimes elaborate proportions. Concealed storage compartments for weapons, gear, or written communications, hidden passageways from room to room or from inside the house to the outside, and secret ladders or tunnels for escape were

59. Secret passageway.

cleverly built into what appeared to be ordinary farmhouses. Unique construction methods that employed optical illusions permitted some ninja houses to contain entire hidden rooms. Other homes had specially mounted walls that could pivot or quickly swing open and shut to allow a ninja to escape from intruders, and floors that would emit warning sounds or give way when stepped on by the unsuspecting. Total precaution was the way of life for the ninja espionage agent, and his home was designed to be the ultimate sanctuary.

60. Ninja armor for battlefield protection.

COMMANDO TACTICS

Another strong point of the ninja warrior was his ability to assume an active role in combat after his espionage skills were no longer useful. Though the ninja did occasionally serve with the regular forces in battle, his primary military value was that of a commando or guerrilla fighter, striking unexpectedly in small numbers using unorthodox tactics.

In the year 1487, a *chunin* from Iga named Ando Kawai and his *genin* were instrumental in the military victory of Shogun

Yoshihisa Ashikaga over Takayori Rokkaku. The Ashikaga forces had built a fortress across from the Rokkaku castle, but were unable to accomplish their objectives through conventional combat methods. Yoshihisa then hired the ninja team to assist his soldiers. Ando and his men were successful, and from that point in history on, ninja agents were collectively referred to as *Iga-mono* (men of Iga) in recognition of their unique skills.

Breaching Enemy Lines

Of first importance to the ninja team working as a commando unit was the penetration of enemy lines. The ninja's *heiho* (military strategy) evolved several possible methods of entering enemy territory.

Troop movements or actual assaults were used to divert the attention of the enemy, giving the ninja a chance to move into the enemy's territory or camp. Diversionary tactics were especially effective when the forces of the opposition were spread out over a large area.

The ninja team could split up and disguise themselves as enemy soldiers or natives of the area, in order to pass into territory held by the enemy without causing suspicion. The ninja could also pose as traitors to their own side, offering to sell out to the enemy, or simply hire on as mercenary troops.

The ninja would then find out who the enemy leaders were, where the camps were, and what constituted their strengths and weaknesses. At the appropriate moment the ninja might go into action against the enemy using ambush, fire, or direct attack.

It was often useful to disrupt the enemy's crucial communications network through the use of rumors and interception or falsification of messages. By making the channels of communication unreliable, the ninja could upset the enemy's morale, cause dissent, or turn friends and allies against each other. If communications were not trusted, reports of ninja in the area might go unheeded.

61. A rope technique used to penetrate the enemy fortress.

Penetrating the Stronghold

After the enemy lines had been breached, the new target might be the enemy camp or castle itself. Once inside the ninja could attack with fire or explosives, destroy vital food and water supplies, set traps, or take hostages. However, the enemy stronghold was very difficult to enter because of the concentration of personnel, guards, and animals, and the physical structure of the castle or camp itself. Ninjutsu provided the principles of *ten* (heaven), *chi* (earth), and *jin* (mankind) as guidelines to successful entry of the enemy stronghold. Whether the entire team launched an assault or a single ninja slipped in alone, these three principles steered their activities.

62. Stealing into the stronghold.

The principle of heaven constituted a concern for the timing of the attack. Good times to move into the castle included those moments when the enemy was otherwise occupied. Meal or rest times, the setting up of a new camp, the distribution of supplies, and times when the enemy forces were away scouting or fighting were all opportune for making a raid on the stronghold. Weather conditions could also be of aid. During rain or snow storms, or heavy fogs, visibility and noise perception were reduced in the enemy compound, making attack easier.

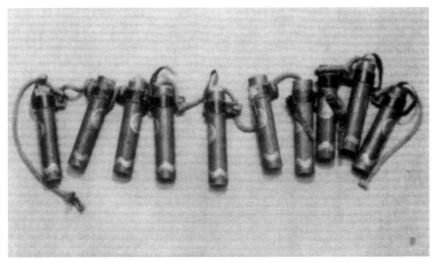

63. Tubes filled with gunpowder, when set off, produced a sound like rifle fire, distracting the enemy.

The earth principle emphasized picking the appropriate weak spot in the enemy's camp or castle, through which there would be the best chance of breaking in. The ninja might pick a dimly lit quarter, an area of much activity and confusion, or an empty hall or room. An appropriate means of entering and then leaving safely had to be chosen, such as disguise, underwater techniques, and so forth.

The principle of mankind taught the ninja to manipulate the human element once inside the enemy's headquarters. The ninja team would make note of the weaknesses of various guards or security procedures to play on these faults. Interesting amusements or peculiar events could be staged to distract the negligent guard, or through the repetition of small noises he might be conditioned to ignore any unusual sounds after searching out a few false alarms. An alert guard might be drawn away from his post by a fire, animal noises, or a feigned or actual attack in another area of the camp.

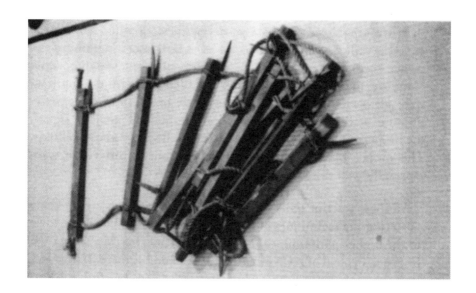

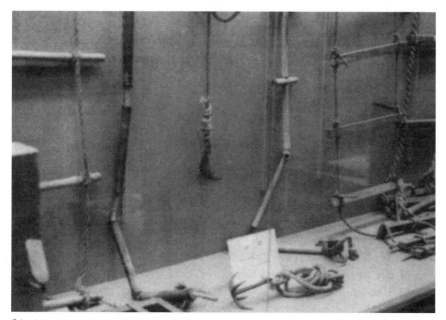

64. (a) Collapsible ladder; (b) a variety of climbing tools used to enter enemy fortifications.

By training the ninja was a master of silent, invisible movement, and this skill was often called on as a last resort in gaining entrance to enemy strongholds. Methods of silent walking, agile climbing, underwater swimming, and blending with the shadows were all particularly useful in the castle or camp of the enemy. Because of the unique construction methods of ancient Japan, the ninja could move undetected beneath floors or above ceilings. The ninja's black outfit and protective but sensitive *tabi* were especially well suited to stealthy movement.

All these warrior skills were perfected by *genin,* who spent years mastering the techniques of combat and espionage but cared little for the higher philosophical and political concepts that concerned the *jonin.* Typical of *genin* were the three Sada brothers, Hikoshiro, Jingoro, and Konezumi, who were retained by the warlord Morishige Hara during the turbulent sixteenth century. They were brilliant but amoral tacticians and tricksters, who always enjoyed the challenge of a job that had been given up as impossible by more conventional thinkers. They were known as masters of concealment, disguise, and hypnotism *(saiminjutsu).*

The Sada brothers occasionally took on ninjutsu students, and one trainee named Sankuro Maruyama decided to sneak into his teachers' house as a test of skill. Moving stealthily through the garden, Sankuro paused to evaluate his surroundings. He suddenly became aware that one of the Sadas had left his bed and was approaching noiselessly, and so he slipped away without completing his self-appointed mission. In the morning Jingoro Sada asked Sankuro if that had been he lurking about at midnight. Sankuro replied yes, and asked how his teacher had known of his presence. Jingoro answered that the insects in the garden had suddenly become silent, so he knew that an intruder was nearby. The teacher then asked his student how he had known to leave before being caught. Sankuro told Jingoro that mosquitos, which are generally quiet at midnight, had suddenly begun buzzing around, warning him that someone had thrown open the mosquito netting to leave his bed. Jingoro commended the student for his attention to detail.

Another tale from the Sada brothers' school of ninjutsu tells of the time when their student Hikotaro Sayama attempted to sneak into the teachers' house in order to steal their furniture as a test of his ability. Hikotaro slipped in through the kitchen entrance, imitating one of the Sadas' dogs in search of fish bones in the garbage to cover any noises that he might make. From the far side of the house, the voice of one of the Sada brothers suddenly boomed out the comment that large dogs chew through fish bones with their mouths three spans above the ground, while this noise was coming from the waist level of a fully grown man. Hikotaro stopped short in amazement and crept away with a higher respect than ever for the ninjutsu prowess of his teachers.

Anyone can learn effective methods of combat and espionage, regardless of motive. Without benign philosophical direction, however, power so easily becomes a tool to promote greed, cruelty, and the domination of others for the sake of personal pleasure. History is littered with stories of men who felt that their own share of happiness would increase proportionally with the sorrow they brought to others.

The mountain mystics of Iga became experts in warfare as a contribution to society. Their power, based on enlightenment, was their gift to the oppressed. When power is guided by proper motivation, as a *genin* was guided by his *jonin,* it is conducive to harmony, fulfillment, and peace in society. This was the commitment of the original Togakure warriors: to dedicate their lives to protecting the innocent who needed their help. For the true ninja, exercising power is the most loving thing he can do.

133

7 ✦ THE REALM OF THE SPIRIT

PSYCHOLOGICAL WARFARE

"The first step to spiritual power is to rid yourself of desire." Hatsumi Sensei's face held an expression of solemn authority. He spoke with conviction.

I was disappointed almost to the point of contempt. Hatsumi Sensei was supposed to be introducing me to the fourth of the nine levels of development, and he had begun with a cliché that I could have gotten from a cheap Hong Kong kung-fu thriller. Rid yourself of desire. How will that help in the real world? How could one develop the power for which the ninja were famous, without desire?

I nodded gamely for the sake of fitting in. "It's a common thing in the States, desire. Everyone wants a big car, a big house with a pool, lots of money," I agreed amicably. After all, the man was my teacher.

There was an odd pause. The master seemed to be looking for words. He tilted his head slightly and continued his explanation. "Well, yes, those are desires. But those desires are superficial and rather easily overcome. What we are talking about are the desires of the personality. Demanding that things be ways they are not."

"Oh, I understand now. It's wanting to be famous, or rich, or powerful," I said.

Hatsumi Sensei smiled wearily. "Well, yes, those are desires, too, but not . . . this is difficult to explain." The master ran a hand over his close-cropped hair. "Let me phrase it this way. You must clear your mind and being of preconceived impressions of the way things are. Many times there is a great difference between what we want to believe and what is real. We can be so caught up in what we want to see, that we are prevented from seeing what is really there. These are the desires that cloud the mind and prevent it from being in touch with the world."

I slowly realized that I had not been allowing the master's words to sink in because of my preconceived notions of what he was saying. I had read his words the way I wanted to, and had missed the meaning entirely.

Hatsumi Sensei went on. "When I say we desire that something be a certain way, I do not necessarily mean that we want it to *be* that way. We want to *think* it is that way. If you think of a certain man as your enemy, then anything he says or does will be examined and found to be an insult or a threat. The identical words or actions on the part of a beloved friend would carry far different meanings. We have a saying: 'Suspicious eyes see only evil.' The unenlightened will see only what they desire to see."

We human beings choose to see things as we wish. Few people seem to believe this, though. We decide to be jealous, or angry, or depressed, or happy, or bored, and these choices are often based on our biased interpretations of the thoughts of others. It is amazing how much psychological control many people relinquish to others. If we think that someone else disapproves of us, we are worried. If we think that someone else is pleased with us, we are happy. If we think that someone else holds views contrary to our own, we are insulted. If we think that someone else is contemptuous of us, we are angry. With all these others determining how we feel, it is sometimes difficult to find the actual self.

"These are the desires of which I speak, these mental barriers that prevent us from accepting fully all that life has to offer. If a man wastes his time in emotional indulgence, he will be forever preoccupied and will miss much that could be his."

"Wouldn't an emotionless life be incredibly dull?" I asked.

"We aren't talking about getting rid of emotions themselves. We are talking about getting rid of inappropriate and useless emotional responses. These uncontrollable responses are weaknesses, in that they make us manipulatable by others."

The ninja's most subtle, and perhaps most insidious, method of handling adversaries is the manipulation of the enemy's mind. One of the highest developments of shadow warfare, the ninja's pragmatic psychology is based on fundamental human weaknesses. By recognizing an adversary's needs and fears, the ninja knows just what to give him or deprive him of in order to bring him to submission. The ninja observes subtle body signals, voice qualities, facial features, and personality quirks in the enemy to know how to manipulate him.

The Five Weaknesses

Just as the ninja interpret physical combat and espionage in terms of the five basic manifestations (see pp. 55, 117), they classify psychological activity in terms of these five. The different manifestations are seen as symbolic representations of the varying levels of consciousness in the human personality.

Chi (earth), the basest grouping of things, shows up as the solid physicality of the body, and is reflected in feelings of stability and resistance to change or movement.

Sui (water), the next higher grouping, is manifest as the fluid aspects of the body, and is reflected in feelings of changeability and emotional reactions to physical changes.

Ka (fire) is seen as the dynamic energy of aggressiveness, and is reflected in feelings of warmth and expansiveness, and the active direction of power and control over one's environment.

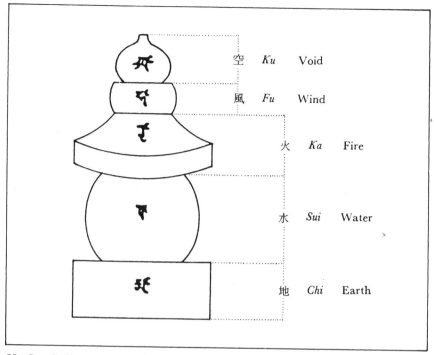

65. Symbolic representation of the five manifestations.

Fu (wind), the highest physical manifestation, displays itself as intellect and love, and is reflected in feelings of wisdom and benevolence, and in conscious consideration of one's interactions with others.

Ku (void), the emptiness of potential, the source of all that is, gives rise to creative capability and the ability to direct the body's energies to take the form of any of the four lower manifestations.

The ninja classified the emotional weaknesses in five basic categories that related to the basic manifestations. Some adversaries almost always react in the same manner, and can be identified with one specific weakness. Others fluctuate from one weakness to another, depending on the circumstances.

137

Laziness. Corresponding to the earth level of consciousness is the weakness of complacency or laziness. Some adversaries will become involved only as much as they are forced to. The lazy or careless often allow their guard to drop through lack of awareness or thoroughness.

Some guards make only a cursory search, and unless something seems outrageously out of place, conclude that all is well in their sector. Through laziness or boredom, this type of adversary is easily overcome by taking a few extra steps to make things a little more difficult and discouraging for him. Idle curiosity can also lure this adversary away from his duties.

In recent wars, interesting psychological tricks have been played using this personality trait. A captured soldier might be given all sorts of luxuries and kind treatment as though they were routine for captured prisoners. After being allowed to escape, the soldier returned to his side with wild stories of his find, reducing the fighting spirit of his comrades and perhaps convincing a few to surrender to the country-club prison camp rather than facing death in the field. Of course, the prisons they found were the real ones—brutal and degrading.

A similar ploy might be used to gain information from soldiers in a prison camp. After a few weeks of imprisonment, some members of a captured group were seen walking about the camp in clean clothes, with a well-fed appearance. These fortunate few wondered why they had been selected for kind treatment, while their deprived friends were told that they had already cooperated and told all they knew. The resulting resentment would be enough to cause a few deprived captives to talk, hoping to get the same rewards.

Anger. This volatile emotion, representing the water level of consciousness, can also be used to control an adversary. In the heat of anger, people often act rashly without thought. An adversary with a short temper could be taken advantage of by inducing him to anger and irrational action. Facing a calm, observant, skilled fighter, the raging, flailing brawler stands little chance of success. His anger will dull his vision and thinking.

To understand anger as a weapon, the student examines himself and others. He learns what causes anger in people. Observation will show that not all people are angered by the same cues. Threats or ridicule may trigger anger in some; impatience or feelings of personal ineptitude may fire others; and some individuals may become enraged when they feel that others are incompetent or have betrayed them. Coming to know the roots of one's own anger promotes understanding of others, and makes one less likely to become a target of those who would rule through the cultivation of anger.

A story is told of a Japanese lord, limited in power and resources, who faced imminent attack from a powerful general's army. The lesser lord appeared relaxed and soothed his staff with the assurance that all would go well, as the attacking general's two chief officers were really henchmen of the lesser lord. Spies in his compound fell for the lies, and carried the names of the "traitors" back to their general. The hotheaded general immediately had the two, in reality quite loyal, officers executed.

Fear. This emotional response comes from the fire level. While in terror, many people will overlook obvious possibilities of countering action or escape. The mild-natured and meek are easily defeated through intimidation tactics. These people are held back by their own lack of confidence or desire to enter into conflict. Fear is the prime weapon of most muggers, rapists, and armed thieves. Through the use of loud profanity, rough actions, and the threat of violence, the attacker can temporarily shock his victim into a state of subservience.

To understand the power of fear as a weapon, one can recall personal experiences of fear or panic. One must objectively examine the situations or cues that brought this emotion to pre-

139

dominance. Many people fear physical pain or the possibility of injury. Some fear the idea of appearing foolish, inadequate, or weak. For others, being alone, helpless, or insecure may bring on the grip of fear. And there are the countless personal fears of specific environmental aspects, the phobias, which must be taken into consideration: fear of heights, confinement, deep water, bees, snakes, foreigners, sharp objects, and so on. Learning to come to grips with one's own fears gives insight into the fears of others. Like anger, fear cannot be totally eliminated from the personality. One can, however, lessen its immobilizing effects by examining those things that cause it, and developing confidence in areas where one feels threatened.

With some adversaries, reputation alone is enough to inspire fear and reluctance for combat. In preparing to fight, a man might have doubts as to the wisdom of his action if he heard that he was facing someone who had killed four others in hand-to-hand combat, or someone with powerful and intimidating friends.

Sympathy. Those with an exaggerated wind level of personality, the softhearted and overly sympathetic, can be manipulated by appealing to their tenderness. By inspiring pity in an adversary, the ninja can disguise his true objectives. Underestimating or ignoring a potential adversary because of his helpless appearance is a milder form of this same emotional indulgence. Many times, ninja of past generations posed as beggars, cripples, or mental incompetents in order to put their adversaries off guard. Swaggering samurai paid scant attention to a wretched little creature incapable of challenging their fighting prowess.

In some cases, pity or softheartedness is a constant state, preventing people from doing anything serious to defend themselves. To these people, knives, guns, finger drives to the eyes, and so forth are too brutal to be used on a fellow human being. Their attackers, however, rarely show much concern for anyone's feelings or well-being. Sympathetic souls are often trapped into handling situations under rules that others do not feel obligated to observe.

Closely related to the feelings of pity or sympathy are those of guilt and obligation. As strong factors in behavioral motivation, guilt and obligation often work even against the adversary's own will. By working to build up feelings of indebtedness in his victim, the ninja wins through the power of self-negation.

One must carefully examine one's own life to come to an understanding of the intricate set of balances and relationships that temper one's outlook on one's fellow man. The teachings of the ninja in no way discourage the feeling of compassion for others. Quite the contrary; the original ninja were very compassionate men. Their spiritual awareness gave them unique insight into the scheme of totality, and their compassion prompted them to act to maintain balance and harmony in the world. For many, however, feelings of compassion are muddied with concerns of "right and wrong" or what is "fair" or "just." The resultant emotion is not true compassion, but a need to do what is satisfying to the self for the sake of feeling "good." It is this forced compassion that can be manipulated to topple an adversary. Perhaps the best summation of the ninja's kindness is an adjusted version of the clichéd golden rule that Western schoolchildren are taught to parrot. The ninja would read it as "Do nothing to others that you would not have them do to you."

Vanity. This complex emotion, which corresponds to the creative awareness born of the void, can be effectively used against an adversary. A vain or overly confident person often does not realize who his enemies are. An overriding concern for oneself is sometimes accompanied by a lack of sensitivity to others, and reasons for feelings of hostility or resentment in others may be overlooked. The person who does not realize when others are working for his downfall is in an extremely vulnerable position. In its most elementary form, vanity can manifest itself in concern for prestige, ego gratification, or appearance. This weakness can be catered to with flattery and feigned friendship, love, respect, or adoration. Any action that feeds the adversary's ego brings him that much closer, and lowers his guard that much more. The vain or self-centered can in that way be set up for surprise attack, or at the least deception.

A more subtle, but nonetheless precarious, form of vanity is the total commitment to some ideal, concept, or endeavor. This seemingly self-denying passion is really an attachment of the personality to some outside source of gratification. By working along with this adversary's cause (or business, or religion, or beliefs), the ninja can play up to his enemy's feeling that by promoting his endeavor, the ninja is actually promoting him. Sometimes the enemy recognizes this transfer of vanity and works to conceal it by prompting others to work hard for "the faith" or "our" business. In manipulating this adversary's ego, the trick is to cater to his vanity without letting him know that the ninja realizes where his heart truly lies.

The Five Needs

In addition to capitalizing on an adversary's emotional weaknesses, the ninja can manipulate his target's fundamental needs. Like the weaknesses, the needs are placed in five broad categories corresponding to the basic manifestations. By catering to or supplying a need, a ninja can develop a feeling of obligation on the part of the person being cultivated. Later, this debt can be touched upon when the ninja might need assistance or some item of information.

Security. This, corresponding to the earth level of personality, is a strong need of some. Many times ninja cultivated an accomplice by providing food and protection to a hunted or dispossessed man or family. Morality and political ideals dim in importance for many people who are deprived of the fundamental necessities of normal living. On the other side of the coin, threatening the security of a man might bring him to submission.

Sex. In another reliable ploy, the desires of an individual can be catered to by supplying sexual excitement, which works on the water level of the personality. In the midst of lusty physical gratification, an enemy's guard is lowered and he becomes much more vulnerable to physical attack or verbal probing. The use of female ninja was often resorted to when other measures had failed.

Wealth. The ninja can appeal to the fire level of his target by taking advantage of his desire for monetary gain. This is an obvious ploy, summed up by the contemporary observation that "Every man has his price." Paying someone off, or offering him the chance for great wealth, can often be used to inspire at least temporary loyalty.

Pride. A man's own appraisal of his personal worth or significance in the eyes of others springs from the wind level of consciousness, and results in pride. Never to be understimated, pride often causes a man to fight relentlessly against overwhelming odds, even to the death, for the sake of self-image or reputation. The ninja might offer a way to regain lost pride and esteem, or threaten an action that could humiliate a man of prestige, thus bringing him into submission.

Pleasure. In order to gain someone's confidence or cooperation, the ninja attacks the creative and expressive level of the void, by discovering and supplying that which brings him pleasure or fulfillment. Beyond mere security or even wealth, men still seek more, whether it be power, influence, increased enjoyment of life, answers to ageless questions, or the opportunity for personal expression.

Self-knowledge

I asked the master how to drop the desires—just use will power?

Hatsumi Sensei told me that crude suppression of personal needs was the hard way to rid the personality of its vulnerabilities, and not very effective in the long run. The best procedure is to openly and honestly examine those things we think we want, and those things we think we wish to avoid. Many times, the mind tries to protect the "observer" in us from the truth. We learn to hide our true feelings beneath a cover that we feel is more acceptable to others and to our own sense of ourselves. We may want to become teachers or priests, not really for the good we can do, but because we are seeking a feeling of importance or superiority over others. We may desire nice clothes and luxurious living quarters, not for the comfort they bring, but for the fact that they make us look attractive to others. We may seek corporate or political power, not for the obvious rewards, but to make up for feelings of personal inferiority. The examples are endless.

In knowing himself, the ninja can come to an honest appraisal of his weaknesses and those areas where he is vulnerable. From there he must find ways of strengthening the potential trouble areas. He cannot just close his eyes and pretend they do not exist. He must satisfy the needs through personal understanding and work the weaknesses out of his personality.

THE FORCE OF THE KILLER

During a later training session, one of the students asked the master in a polite tone, "What do all these personality aspects have to do with fighting?"

Hatsumi Sensei smiled warmly. "They have to do with not needing to fight." There was a momentary pause while we contemplated the comment.

"There are certain types of conflict where you might not even realize that you have an adversary. You would not even have a chance to fight. How do you fight a sniper armed with a silenced rifle? How do you fight an assassin who stabs you unseen from behind? How do you fight the man who rigs your car to explode when you turn on the ignition?"

The teachers present kept their gaze on the master. They seemed to know the answers. The rest of us shifted around uneasily and looked at each other with questioning glances.

Hatsumi Sensei broke the silence. "There is no way that you can fight him." It was not the answer I had been hoping to hear.

"Since you cannot successfully fight this adversary, you must learn to protect yourself in other ways. The ninja refines his perceptive abilities to a level higher than most humans', and becomes sensitive to input from sources in addition to his five physical senses. The ability to perceive what we call 'premonitions of danger' takes the ninja to the fifth of the nine developmental levels.

"An attacker, whether man or animal, puts forth his harmful intentions as a sort of vibration or thought impulse. Just as we say that sights, smells, or sounds are things, we can also say that thoughts are things. The ninja refers to these thought impulses that accompany harmful intentions as *sakki* [the force of the killer]. This *sakki* is there to be perceived, regardless of whether or not we are sensitive enough to pick it up.

"When you are sensitive enough to detect this intention of harmful action, you can fight back by simply not being where the attack will take place."

I asked the master, "How can you tell the perception of the killer's force from mere fear or paranoia?"

"You must learn to trust your perception, by working to develop it as a skill. And when the proper time arrives, we can test the student's ability to recognize premonitions of harm."

"How can you test something that you cannot see?" I asked.

"We can only check the results. Let me show you the test. It is really very simple."

145

Hatsumi Sensei motioned for one of the teachers to move to the center of the training area. The teacher turned his back to the master and slowly assumed the *seiza* (traditional Japanese sitting position), with legs tucked beneath him and hands resting on thighs. His eyes seemed to be half-closed and his breathing pace was relaxed.

The master picked up a bamboo training sword and moved to a position behind the sitting teacher. His movements were silent, and the teacher seemed to be totally unaware of the figure behind him. The sword was constructed of four split bamboo sticks tied together in a narrow bundle. Leather caps at both ends held the strips of bamboo together. The master slowly raised this nasty-looking weapon above his head.

The master held his pose with sword uplifted, while the teacher remained in the sitting position. They were perfectly still, and resembled a scene in a wax museum. The rest of the students watched intently, as a heavy silence enveloped the training hall. Seconds passed quietly.

The scene suddenly exploded. It was as though I were watching a film with several frames removed, causing the characters to suddenly jump into new poses. Hatsumi Sensei's face momentarily tightened, and then he brought the sword straight down at the teacher's head. Instantly the teacher rolled away from the strike, just before the sword tip smashed into the floor with a boom. There had been no perceptible warning or noise, and the sword had cut straight through the space previously occupied by the sitting teacher.

The whole thing was over in a split second. I tried to remember some sort of clue—a foot tap, a little cough, or a rattle of the sword to warn the teacher. I had not seen the tip-off, if it had been a trick.

Another teacher took his place sitting in the center of the room. The master again assumed a ready position behind the new victim. I decided that it must have been some sort of timed count that had allowed the first teacher to escape. My theory was shattered along with the silence in the training hall as the sword again crashed into the wooden floor. The second teacher barely had time to get settled before he went rolling away from the attack.

The demonstration was set up again with a third teacher who sat in the center of the training area. Again the sword descended, and again I saw a black-robed body slipping away from the unseen danger in a fraction of a second.

The demonstration was the first occasion on which I had ever noticed an expression of violence or anger on the face of Hatsumi Sensei. It seemed very unlike him and made me uncomfortable. Each time the sword began its downward swing, the master's face clouded fiercely as though he really wanted to hurt the teacher.

The master laughed when he heard my thoughts. "Of course I intended to hurt them. That intention is what triggered their movement. If I had not really meant to hurt them, there would have been no *sakki* for them to perceive, and no danger to avoid. This perception is difficult to master, and no mere trick. The test has to be the real thing. You have enrolled to study a method of self-protection for life-or-death situations. You are not playing a sport or game."

I asked one of the teachers in the demonstration how he had been able to avoid the strike. I wanted to know how he could tell when the sword was on its way.

He nodded his head and thought for a moment. A serious look came across his face. He finally looked at me and said that he did not know how he had done it. He had simply had a peculiar feeling that he needed to move. It had not been a thought as such, he told me. It had been more a physical sensation in his body. He had just felt that he must move.

The master later explained that the ability to perceive potential danger is developed by learning how to tune into a level of thought higher than routine individual consciousness. Just as we all share a common realm of visual perceptions, tactile stimulations, and sound impulses, we share a range of higher frequencies that is affected by thought impulses. If we are sensitive enough we can utilize this sixth sense just as we utilize sight, or taste, or hearing.

Acknowledging perceptions received through this sense is difficult at first, obviously. It is hard enough to get people to agree on interpretations of even base physical sensations. Any given room contains a certain degree of heat, and yet people will disagree as to whether the room is too hot or too cold. Two men might view the same fabric, reflecting only one pattern of light waves, and argue as to whether it is green or blue. Certain sounds might be musical to one person, and painful to another. An even more difficult task is getting people to agree on their interpretations of the actions of others. Different acquaintances might think of the same person as exciting, pitiful, irrational, comical, wise, and so on, depending on their own frames of reference. Which of course brings us back to the original lesson—getting rid of those desires that make up our limiting frames of reference. We need to rid ourselves of the psychological and emotional obstacles that prevent us from clearly receiving all the subtle input coming to us.

That is the point of working to know oneself. It is not for the sake of merely being a nice person. One must strive to clear away all the twisted, faulty perceptions—all the mental noise and contradictions that take up so much psychic energy. It is hard work. We must undo all the programming from decades of trying to fit in. But the rewards are great. Once we have cleared away the jungle of desires that has grown up around our observing processes, we are on the way to spiritual power. We are cleaned and open to new input. We have taken the first step toward understanding and working through the universal scheme of totality. That is the ninja's world.

66. In (yin) and yo (yang).

THE GREAT HARMONY

In moving beyond the fifth level of development, the ninja cultivates further powers of the mind by increasing his sensitivity to the harmony inherent in the universe. This harmony is the product of the constant balancing relationship of *in* and *yo*, which can be understood as the basic polar extremes of the universe, or as the concepts of female and male on a cosmic scale. The Chinese write of *yin* and *yang*, the Judeo-Christian tradition speaks of Heaven and Earth, and the Western scientific world uses the concept of positive and negative to describe the same process. The *in* is seen in the dark, heavy, finite, wet, contracting, and lunar. The *yo* is manifest in the bright, light, infinite, dry, expansive, and solar.

To understand this interaction, the ninja looks at the universe as a single, ever-moving process, rather than as countless isolated objects or actions. On the surface, this seems difficult to do. The earth itself, let alone the entire universe, is so vast that our limited human physical senses are incapable of seeing or understanding its entirety. A given human being in his universe could be compared to a photon in an atom. That photon has no way of seeing that it is part of an atom, which is part of an element, which in

149

combination with other elements may make up some part in the engine of an automobile. Even more incomprehensible to that photon is the fact that someone may be using the automobile to transport himself to, say, a place of employment. The average human being is equally unconscious of his role in the total process of the universe. The best he can do is look around and be aware of all the other pieces around him. And so we classify things as mountains, laughter, tangerines, pain, clouds, stars, and so on. The scope of seeing all this as one thing is beyond us, and to some people even seems preposterous.

However, those of us who refuse to even consider the universe as one integral process probably view all things beneath us as integral processes without realizing it. We climb into an automobile and drive away totally unconscious of its countless independent parts and events. Valves rise and release gases, feet apply varying pressures to pedals, shafts revolve, that photon buzzes about its atom, liquids flow, and so many things go on that it is virtually impossible to be conscious of them all at the same instant. So we merely refer to the whole process as "driving" and let it go at that.

It is a matter of proportion and perspective. Sometimes we are too small to see the process, so we see only a few of the parts. Sometimes we are too big to see the parts, so we see only the process. This relativity is concisely captured by the ancient concepts of *in* and *yo*. The things or processes themselves are not inherently *in* or *yo*, or positive, negative, long, hot, small, good, evil, or anything else. Any quality that we ascribe to a thing is an appraisal of its relationship to other things. We call something small because there are larger things to compare it with. A silver dollar is a small disk next to two hubcaps. It becomes a big coin alongside three dimes, however. Hypodermic needles may be considered bad by the coughing child being injected; however, the physician sees his act as one of benefit to a sick person. Two hundred dollars can be a lot of money or a little, depending on whether you are buying a camp stove or an automobile. And what is called sin in one religion might be the key to enlightenment and salvation in another.

A common misconception is to regard the *in* and *yo* as opposites in all cases. This explanation is perhaps given to simplify the presentation to people unfamiliar with the *in-yo* balancing concept. However, the opposites we normally think of are not always the most accurate. The opposite of love is not hate, but rather complete indifference. The opposite of bitterness is not sweetness, but rather blandness, the lack of taste. The ninja comes to realize that the conflict of dualism is not the most efficient way of regarding things.

Once we learn how to recognize the universe as an integral process comprising an infinite number of parts, we can begin to rid ourselves of feelings of isolation or separateness. This great mental step is a clearing away of the negative me-against-the-world attitude that is encouraged by so many of the world's societies, religions, and cultures. Once we realize that we are working parts of the process, we free ourselves from the notion that we are mere victims in life, taunted by gods and devils, buffeted helplessly between poles of good luck and bad luck. The ninja then works to gain insight as to how he can guide the universal process to accomplish his will, or tap it as universal consciousness to gain knowledge.

By mastering the mental abilities of the fourth through sixth levels, the ninja lays the foundation for progress to the true realm of the spirit, on the seventh level and above. It is these advanced levels of power that are said to give the ninja "the mind and eyes of God."

✦ GLOSSARY-INDEX

155

The Ninja and Their Secret Fighting Art

2017年 5月 31日　第1刷発行

著　者　ステファン・K・ヘイズ

発行者　エリック・ウイ

発行所　チャールズ・イー・タトル出版

〒141-0032 東京都品川区大崎5-4-12 八重苅ビル3F

電話 03-5437-0171 Email: sales@tuttle.co.jp

ISBN 978-4-8053-1430-2 Printed in Singapore